Kurt Blaukopf on Music Sociology – an Anthology

Musik und Gesellschaft

Herausgegeben von Alfred Smudits

Band 31

PL ACADEMIC RESEARCH

Tasos Zembylas (ed.)

Kurt Blaukopf on Music Sociology – an Anthology

2nd Unrevised Edition

PL ACADEMIC RESEARCH

Bibliographic Information published by the Deutsche Nationalbibliothek
The Deutsche Nationalbibliothek lists this publication in the Deutsche Nationalbibliografie; detailed bibliographic data is available in the internet at http://dnb.d-nb.de.

Library of Congress Cataloging-in-Publication Data
Names: Blaukopf, Kurt. | Zembylas, Tasos, editor. | Westacott, David, translator. | Marinelli, David, translator.
Title: Kurt Blaukopf on music sociology : an anthology / Tasos Zembylas (ed.); translation by David Westacott and David Marinelli.
Description: 2nd unrevised edition. | New York : Peter Lang, 2016. | Series: Musik und Gesellschaft ; Band 31 | Includes bibliographical references.
Identifiers: LCCN 2016025311 | ISBN 9783631675724
Subjects: LCSH: Musicology—Methodology. | Weber, Max, 1864-1920. | Music—Social aspects.
Classification: LCC ML3797 .B534 2016 | DDC 306.4/842—dc23 LC record available at https://lccn.loc.gov/2016025311

Cover image:
© Tasos Zembylas

Translation by David Westacott and David Marinelli

The translation has generously been funded by the Austrian Science Fund (FWF) and the University of Music and Performing Arts Vienna"

F ШF

Der Wissenschaftsfonds.

mdw
universität
für musik und
darstellende
kunst wien

ISSN 0259-076X
ISBN 978-3-631-67572-4 (Print)
E-ISBN 978-3-653-07110-8 (E-Book)
DOI 10.3726/978-3-653-07110-8

© Peter Lang GmbH
Internationaler Verlag der Wissenschaften
Frankfurt am Main 2012
2nd unrevised Edition 2016.
All rights reserved.
PL Academic Research is an Imprint of Peter Lang GmbH.

Peter Lang – Frankfurt am Main · Bern · Bruxelles · New York · Oxford · Warszawa · Wien

This publication has been peer reviewed.

www.peterlang.com

Table of contents

Preface   7

Part I – On the Foundation of Music Sociology   **11**

Goals of the Sociology of Music   13

Music Praxis as the Subject of Sociology   21

Part II – On Max Weber's Sociology of Music   **37**

Max Weber and Music Sociology   39

The Concept of Progress in Music Sociology   51

Part III – Mediamorphosis   **61**

The Mediamorphosis of Music as Global Phenomenon   63

Part IV – Sociology and the Philosophy of Science   **93**

The Sociological Concept of the *Kunstwollen* and
its Origins in the Austrian School of Art History
and Musicology   95

The Sociology of Art in the Orchestra of the Sciences   109

On Kurt Blaukopf   **121**

Biographical Notes on Kurt Blaukopf 1914–1999   123
Michael Parzer

Appendix   **145**

Selected list of publications of Kurt Blaukopf   147

The Kurt Blaukopf Archive in Vienna   150

Copyright permissions   151

Preface

This anthology contains seven texts by Kurt Blaukopf (1914-1999), which were published over the last 40 years, mostly in German. They exemplify the sociological and epistemological position of this pioneer of Austrian music sociology. Blaukopf's efforts were aimed at a comprehensive, interdisciplinary approach and analysis of music as a cultural phenomenon and as social practice. He recognised that music sociology often rather concerned itself with the general conditions of music, but at the same time he warned that music sociology should not lose sight of music as a creative practice and as a work of art.

Blaukopf's passion for music is rooted in his biography. He grew up in Vienna in a middle-class Jewish family, and although he followed his father's wish and studied jurisprudence his intellectual attention was devoted to music. From the early 1930s he did extended studies in musicology but at the same time he was deeply aware of the social roots of music, and thus he enriched his approach to music with insights from Max Weber's writings. However, the rise of Nazism in Germany and the Wehrmacht's invasion of Austria forced the young man to leave Vienna. During the years in exile he continued his informal studies in music sociology, but he also became increasingly interested in the epistemological foundations of his own ideas on the subject.

I believe it is no exaggeration to state that Kurt Blaukopf represents the solid Austrian scientific tradition that began with Bernard Bolzano's and Ernst Mach's philosophy of science in the late 19th century. This tradition had been incorporated by some exponents of the Vienna school of art history (Alois Riegl) and musicology (Guido Adler) and developed further by the members of the Vienna Circle and especially in the social sciences by Otto Neurath. Usually described as positivism, the tradition is characterised by a strong reservation towards highly abstract and speculative theories. Furthermore there is a programmatic commitment to fluid boundaries and to linking different specialist disciplines.

These three elements – the Vienna school of art history and musicology, Max Weber's sociology of music and the Austrian philosophy of science – are the epistemological pillars of Blaukopf's intellectual development. The reader will immediately recognise them, as they were determining for Blaukopf's own understanding of the aim of music sociology, namely, the "collection of all the social facts relevant to musical practice, the ordering of these facts according to their significance for musical practice and the recording of the changes of facts that decide practice".[1] The ideal of positivism, namely normative neutrality, distinguishes both Blaukopf's writing style as well as his intentions. "The taste judgements and preferences of the sociologist must remain separate . . . for him, what counts is the proud motto of Spinoza: I do not condemn nor praise; I merely study."[2] In line with this idea of neutrality, Blaukopf exercised a remarkable openness and an interest in different forms of music from different cultural realms and epochs, which extended to contemporary phenomena such as pop music and experimental music. Being a creative person, Blaukopf discovered new topics and therefore he can justifiably be called a pioneer of Austrian music sociology. In the texts selected for this anthology he investigates fundamental questions on the development of music, highlights the role of media and technology, and discusses the link between music and cultural policy. Additionally, he argues against theories of determinism (e.g. sociological Marxism) and goes along with Max Weber's call for sensitivity to the subtle embedding of music in society. Blaukopf finally argues that music sociology must aim for interdisciplinarity and a higher musicological competence.

Kurt Blaukopf was a man who had first-hand experience of the historical developments that had a formative influence on central Europe in the 20th century. His sociological approach to music often indirectly reflects this background.[3] He searches for the innumerable and manifold relations between music and society – and especially the sociography of musical life – constantly aware that music is not determined by societal effects in a narrow sense. However, it is interesting to mention that the effects of Blaukopf's scientific commitment extended beyond the sphere of academia. He also involved himself both as a member of the executive

---

1   Kurt Blaukopf, "Musik", in Wilhelm Bernsdorf / Friedrich Bülow (eds.), *Wörterbuch der Soziologie* (Stuttgart: 1955), 342–346.
2   Kurt Blaukopf, "Patterns of musical behaviour", manuscript in German and English, 1977, 18.
3   Fortunately, Blaukopf himself took stock of his impressive life and intellectual development in an autobiography titled *Unterwegs zur Musiksoziologie* (Graz / Vienna: 1998).

council of Unesco and as an expert in Austrian cultural policy, and he demanded the achievement of two central aims: the democratisation of culture through the improvement of public access and the participation of the whole population in cultural life, as well as the safeguarding and improvement of the economic and social situation of artists.

One of the primary aims of this anthology is to make Blaukopf's work better known in the English-speaking world. It offers the interested reader:

- first, with regard to the history of ideas, an exciting and fruitful analysis of the relation between music sociology and its sister disciplines, for example musicology
- second, a solid reflection in terms of the philosophy of science on the possibilities and limits of music-sociology research, and
- third, after the end of Bourdieu's era, a highly topical discussion about the significance of intrinsic artistic aspects in music sociology. This issue should be highlighted, not just because alongside the general conditions of music Kurt Blaukopf also emphasised the importance of the praxis, but also because he was a music expert who was successful as a writer on music. (His Mahler biography should be mentioned, for example – for 40 years considered a standard work, translated into several languages and reprinted this year.)

In this sense, the anthology touches both on the interest of scholars researching the history of ideas as well as the interest in currently relevant and widely discussed issues, such as the question of mediamorphosis, the sociological analysis of artworks and the sociological explanation of artistic processes of creation.

Editing Blaukopf's texts I was confronted with several details that forced me to make a few changes or textual interventions.

The translation by David Westacott is in British English; the two passages from the already published volume *Musical Life in a Changing Society* with the titles "Goals of the Sociology of Music" and "The Mediamorphosis of Music as a Global Phenomenon" were published in the early 1990s, translated by David Marinelli in US English. As a result there are two different styles in this anthology. Apart from the elimination of minor mistakes in the bibliographical references, I have made only one change to the original texts: in both texts we have replaced the key term *Musiksoziologie*, which was given there as "socio-musicology", with "music sociology". The reasons for this are simple: on the one hand I wanted to assist the reader's understanding, on the other the term "music sociology" has in the meantime become internationally established.

Please note also that the structure of the references and literature differs. All apart from the two texts already translated into US English have footnotes – that is, in the original, Kurt Blaukopf put all bibliographical references in the footnotes. The texts from *Musical Life in a Changing Society* use a different reference system: the bibliographical references are incorporated in abbreviated form in the main text and there is a complete bibliography at the end of each text.

The translation of some terms is not always unambiguous. Thus in some cases I have added editorial notes. These can be found either in square brackets in the main text or in the footnotes.

This anthology has been prepared within few months. I would not have been able to fulfil this task without the help and advice of David Binder, Michael Parzer and Alfred Smudits, who deserve my thanks.

Tasos Zembylas

Part I
On the Foundation of Music Sociology

Goals of the Sociology of Music[1]

From time to time, one must return to investigate words;
for the world can move away while words stand still.
— Georg Christoph Lichtenberg

Thus words too serve to express new ideas
without changing their orthography.
— Emile Durkheim

As a rule, one attempts to circumscribe the field of the sociology of music by starting with the idea, which must be defined more exactly, of how sociology should treat certain aspects of music. Assuming that existing disciplines already deal adequately with several aspects of music (for example, music theory, musical aesthetics, psychology of music, and so on) the only way to legitimize the sociology of music would be to describe its methods and area of application in such a way that its particular task is identified. For many years I regarded this as superfluous, because in my opinion every method of dealing with music involves sociological aspects, and a separate sociology of music could be justified as a "transient science" only as long as scholarship did not integrate it into musicology. I soon revised this interpretation (Blaukopf 1972, 5-6), because theory and methodology (primarily that of the empirical sociology of music) had evolved and become more refined, as reflected in an extensive literature on the subject (cf. Kneif 1966, Elste 1975).

To be sure, that dubious tendency which, over the last thirty years, has been called "the fight for a place in the academic sun" (Acham 1979, 135) has also been responsible for the claim of music sociology to recognition as a separate discipline. This trend should not be supported. On the contrary, we would do well to assign no more than a modest place to the sociology of music, because establishing it as a special area of study carries with it two potential dangers.

---

1   Editorial note: first published in *Musik im Wandel der Gesellschaft: Grundzüge der Musiksoziologie* (Munich: 1982), 15–22. This English version is translated by David Marinelli and published in *Musical Life in a Changing Society: Aspects of Music Sociology* (Portland: 1992), 1–6.

The *first* danger is that sociology may operate with its own ready-made categories, failing to regard music, the object of its research, as the criterion for their usefulness. According to some scholars, sociology concerns itself solely with studying the social involvement of art, and this study cannot be used to "explain the nature and essence of the arts themselves" (Silbermann 1973, 20). Adorno correctly pointed out that this process neglects the actual object and that, in so doing, academic sociology tries to get around methodological difficulties by "classifying in agenda style." In Silbermann's opinion, sociology "has to do with the social effects of music, not with music itself" (Adorno 1976, 196). This type of music sociology, carried out in anything but splendid isolation, operates according to a method that not only is regarded as largely fruitless by musicology but has long since lost validity in sociology as well. Talcott Parsons has indicated that "*every* important empirical field of social science is a field of application for the conceptual schemes of all the relevant theoretical disciplines. No academic organization of the disciplines can overcome this inherent logical cross- and inter-penetration. In which disciplinary category a given empirical field is predominantly placed is usually mainly a matter of historical accident and pragmatic convenience, not of scientific principle" (Parsons 1948, 329).

Gunnar Myrdal addressed himself in a similar fashion to the strict divisions between the various social sciences, emphasizing that "in reality there are not economic, sociological, or psychological problems, but simply problems, and as a rule, they are complex" (Myrdal 1969, 10). Every sociology of art and music seems therefore to demand an interdisciplinary approach, for "a division of labor between disciplines such as philosophy, sociology, psychology, and history is not contained in the subject but is imposed on it from the outside" (Adorno 1967, 101).

The *second* danger in detaching the sociology of music from the music itself is that the dialogue between disciplines may be suppressed, and the long-established disciplines may imagine that sociological reflection on music is no longer within their purview. If a separate discipline already exists to deal with the sociological aspects of music, it might be argued that musicology need not concern itself with the task. In this case, establishing the sociology of music as a separate discipline would stifle the interdisciplinary investigations demanded by the subject itself. Of course, this risk has gradually become less acute. Musicologists such as Guido Adler and Jules Combarieu long ago acknowledged the sociological dimension of their discipline, and the rapid development of comparative musicology and ethnomusicology since the end of the nineteenth century has sensitized musicologists not only to anthropology but to sociology as well.

Musics as Types of Social Activity

These developments have also paved the way for a new definition of the term *music*. For a long time, the definition took as its primary point of departure the concept of music as a work of art. A typical example is the definition given as late as 1961 by the most prestigious German encyclopedia of music: "Music is the artistic discipline whose material consists of sounds" (Musik in Geschichte und Gegenwart, 9/1965, 970). This definition is derived from a preconceived idea of "art" rather than from the verifiable phenomena of musical activity, which extend far beyond art music. A definition of this kind says little about the phenomenon of music, while saying a great deal about a musicology that is preoccupied with art music. Recent musicological literature goes beyond the restrictions inherent in this definition. There is a growing awareness that we cannot speak simply of "music" but must speak instead about various types of "musics" and about differing historical structures of musical behavior. Studies of the development of European folk music and of pre-Renaissance European music, analyses of the technologically disseminated popular music of modern indu strial civilization, and explorations of the musical life of non-European peoples seem to indicate that the subject of musicological research – and therefore the sociology of music – must be defined in a different, more comprehensive way.

All the above considerations direct attention to types of musical behavior that can be regarded as social behavior. (By behavior we mean the observable acts and omissions of people.) Sociology seeks to identify patterns of cultural behavior because these patterns reveal the behavior expectations characteristic of each social structure. The sociology of music is properly concerned with cultural types of behavior, too, for these rules are considered binding for musical behavior as well.

The task of the sociology of music – in keeping with a basic idea of Max Weber's – is to understand musical activity as a social activity, thereby explaining how it originated. Defined in the broadest sense, a *musical activity* is any activity directed toward the production of sound-events intended for others. While this definition is broad enough to include everything – the acoustic utterances of cavemen as well as the writing of a modern score, the repetition of traditional musical formulas as well as the performance of a *res facta* – it is too broad because it also includes all verbal communication, which would contradict our current knowledge as well as the conventional terminology resulting from that knowledge. We are accustomed to distinguishing between the aesthetic information conveyed by music and the semantic information reserved for speech. In our minds, music and speech are separate spheres. Furthermore, this definition of musical activity would lead to problems in defining what we – and all cultures – generally call musical behavior.

Semantic and Aesthetic Information

The problems in defining musical behavior can be overcome by taking into consideration that the logical separation of aesthetic and semantic information (Moles 1968, 124-125) came about relatively recently, whereas both elements were originally linked. In most African cultures, for example, it is impossible to separate the "purely musical" from the spiritual, terpsichorean, and linguistic elements. In these societies, "understanding music" means reacting to music in a culturally defined fashion, which usually includes a dance reaction as well (Nketia 1975, 11-12). Since music is not detached from speech communication and gestural expression, these societies usually lack words that correspond to our idea of "music": Most African languages do not have a word wholly equivalent to the Western term "music." The terms used often mean a combination of music and dance. We frequently find expressions for "song" and "singing" on the one hand and for "dance," "type of dance" and "type of music" on the other (Kubik 1973, 172-173). This close connection between linguistic-semantic and musical-aesthetic communication has also been stressed in studies on the culture of ancient Greece. Although the word *music* is derived from the Greek *musiké,* the two terms actually have little to do with one another. "It is incorrect to translate musiké with music; these two terms designate different things" (Georgiades 1954, 7). *Musiké* is the name for something which we would today regard as a joining of poetry and music: "Ancient Greek verse was a curious form, for which there is no analogy in the Occident. It was, so to say, music and poetry in one; and it is precisely for this reason that it cannot be broken down into the two tangible components of music and poetry" (Georgiades 1954, 6).

The history of the words *musiké* and *music* clearly demonstrates how the function of an expression changes and to what extent it can be filled with new content. In Arab cultures, for example, until the nineteenth century the term *musiqa* was reserved for theoretical treatises on music theory, tonal systems, musical instruments, the aesthetics of music, and so on (Touma 1975, 28). In this instance, then, the word designates not musical practice but theoretical reflection about music.

All scholarly consideration of non-European and ancient European cultures must therefore pay attention to the indivisible connection between linguistic, gestural, and musical elements. When we speak of music in these areas, we must be aware that we are making a mental distinction that does not, in general, exist in either social practice or the thought associated with it. Is it then meaningful, in such instances to speak of music? Yes, but only if we mentally view the isolated musical forms of behavior in conjunction with the predominant types of cultural behavior associated with them.

Musical Practice

This, albeit rather major, limitation will enable us to use the terms *types* of musical behavior, *patterns* of musical behavior (i.e. rules of behavior), and musical behavior *expectations.* Classifying these three concepts under the term musical *practice,* allows us to define the sociology of music as "the compilation of all social data relevant to musical practice, the classification of this data according to its importance for musical practice, and the recording of data of crucial significance in altering practices" (Blaukopf in Bernsdorf / Bülow 1955, 342). This description of music sociology stresses *practice* and the *change* of practice. Rather than starting from music as a work of art, a phenomenon that appeared later in history, it takes as its point of departure music as a social activity, something older than notated music that eventually brought forth the "musical work of art" at a given stage of socio-technological development. (Of course, the composition of such a work of art at this stage is, in its turn, also part of musical practice.) I would like to note again that the word *practice* should not be taken in the narrow sense of referring only to "what is actually heard." It should be extended to include all musical acts and omissions, as well as observable behavior patterns. Theoretical reflection on this musical practice – that is, thought about music based on each practice and capable of influencing it – will also be considered part of this practice of music sociology.

Another important aspect of the foregoing definition is the special attention devoted to the changes in musical practice. As a rule – to which there are, of course, possible exceptions – the sociology of music is unable to explain all parts of a given musical practice from a sociological point of view. It can, however, localize social data which make a given musical practice possible or directly cause it to change. In short, *the sociology of music explains, not why musical practice is the way it is, but how it changes.*

The curious onlooker who expects the sociology of music to "explain" why a certain composer is a great genius will be disappointed, and rightly so, because although the sociology of music is able to list several of the conditions necessary for this greatness, it is by no means able to account for all of them. Even brilliant philosophical attempts (such as Adorno's) to "decipher" musical works of art "sociologically" are unable to alter this fact. Contrary to our definition of the sociology of music, these efforts – which have been emulated by others, with lesser results – start with the work of art and trace their way back to the social background. The exceptional instances in which this has been successful may reinforce the false impression that sociology is able to derive the concrete form of musical artworks from the structure of the society in which these works were created. This misunderstanding has recently been fostered by a number of authors trying to reach that goal by following in Adorno's footsteps. The pseudo-sociology used for such efforts largely employs analogy and metaphor as a speculative means of tying social facts to aesthetic phenomena. They tend to ignore Adorno's warning against this method: "Sociological concepts applied to music are not binding when not founded in the music" (Adorno 1959, 11).

Hans Engel also noted in 1965 that a mere linking of artworks and society is unproductive: "Aesthetic speculation and a mere synchronic listing of musical and social data serve no purpose" (Engel 1965, 966). However, Engel also took Max Weber, the founder of the sociology of music in Germany, to task, maintaining that Weber's fragmentary yet fundamental essay on the rational and sociological bases of music, first published in 1921, had produced "no results." Engel overlooked the fact that Weber was not trying, in this or other studies, to establish at any price a correspondence between music and social system but was concerned instead with discovering the conditions under which musical activity changed. Weber focused his attention on the development of tonal systems, on the conflicts inherent in any rationalization of tonal systems, and on the significance of musical instruments for musical practice – all of which make him a pioneer of socio-musicological thought. As I will show, Weber's socio-musicological thought is closely linked to the musicological and aesthetic thought of his age.

Bibliography

Acham, Karl, "Realgeschichte – Geschichtswissenschaft – historische Sozialwissenschaft", in Kurt Salamun (ed.), *Sozialphilosophie als Aufklärung: Festschrift für Ernst Topitsch* (Tübingen: 1979).

Adorno, Theodor W., *Klangfiguren: Musikalische Schriften I.* (Berlin / Frankfurt am Main: 1959).

Adorno, Theodor W., *Ohne Leitbild: Parva Aesthetica* (Frankfurt am Main: 1967).

Adorno, Theodor W., *Introduction to the Sociology of Music* (New York: 1976).

Bernsdorf, Wilhelm/ Bülow, Friedrich (eds.), *Wörterbuch der Soziologie* (Stuttgart: 1955).

Blaukopf, Kurt, "Hymnen", *HiFi-Sterophonie,* 8/1972, 708.

Elste, Martin, *Verzeichnis deutsprachiger Musiksoziologie 1848-1973* (Hamburg: 1975).

Georgiades, Thrasybulos, *Musik und Sprache: Das Werden der abendländischen Musik* (Berlin: 1954).

Engel, Hans, "Soziologie der Musik", *Musik in Geschichte und Gegenwart* (MGG), 12/1965, 948-967.

Kneif, Tibor, "Gegenwartsfragen der Musiksoziologie: Ein Forschungsbericht", *Acta Musicologica,* 38/1966, 72-118.

Kubik, Gerhard, "Verstehen in afrikanischen Musikkulturen", in Peter Faltin / Hans-Peter Reinecke (eds.), *Musik und Verstehen* (Cologne: 1973).

Moles, Abraham, *Information Theory and Esthetic Perception* (Urbana: 1968)

Myrdal, Gunnar, *Objectivity in Social Research* (Middletown: 1969).

Nketia, Joseph H. Kwabena, "Understanding African Music", *National Centre for the Performing Arts Quarterly Journal*, 4/1975, 8-14

Parsons, Talcott, "The Position of Sociological Theory", paper read at the American Sociological Society, New York, December 1947, in *Synopsis* (Heidelberg: 1948).

Silbermann, Alphons, *Empirische Kunstsoziologie: Eine Einführung mit kommentierter Bibliographie* (Stuttgart: 1973).

Touma, Habib Hassan, *Die Musik der Araber* (Wilhelmshaven: 1975).

Music Praxis as the Subject of Sociology[1]

The demand that research into the arts should be devoted not simply to the works but to the totality of people's dealings with the arts was raised by a man who has gone down in history as a statistician, as a philosopher of science and a Rilke scholar: Richard von Mises (1883–1953) stated that the task of arts research was "to describe and to classify the observable phenomena in the area of art practice and to comprehend their connections with other facts of the individual and social life (as part of psychology and sociology)".[2]

Following the pattern of the phrase "art practice" that Mises uses, one could form the term "music practice". Because the word "practice" perhaps suggests something different in connection with music, I prefer to use the term "music praxis" in precisely the sense that Mises ascribes to "art practice", namely for all kinds of dealings with music. For the rest, too, the following remarks are also oriented on the considerations of Richard von Mises. I owe the initial stimulus for this to Robert Reichardt, who contributed essentially to the understanding of the changes in music praxis in the 20th century with a study of the cultural and economic role of the record.[3]

Music Sociology

1.   Music sociology is the collection of all social facts relevant to changes in music praxis, the ordering of these facts according to their significance for the changes under investigation.

2.   Music consists of *sound events consciously produced by people*.

2.1   Not all sound events of this kind can be classed as music. Acoustic signals that primarily serve to convey linguistic infor-

---

1   Editorial note: the manuscript was written in 1969 and it was first published in a slightly modified version in Michael Benedikt / Reinhold Knoll / Kurt Lüthi (eds.), *Über Gesellschaft hinaus: Kultursoziologische Beiträge im Gedenken an Robert Heinrich Reichardt* (Klausen-Leopoldsdorf: 2000), 145-161.

2   Richard von Mises, *Positivism: A Study in Human Understanding* (New York: 1956), 312.

3   Robert Reichardt, *Die Schallplatte als kulturelles und ökonomisches Phänomen: Ein Beitrag zum Problem der Kunstkommerzialisierung* (Zurich:1962).

mation are just as little to be considered music as for example the acoustic side-effects of an otherwise quite consciously designed work process.

2.11 The appearance of an *acoustic element as an end in itself* serves as the criterion to distinguish musical sound events from other consciously produced sound events. It is a question of music when the sound event contains elements that go beyond the immediate practical ends of its production.

2.12 The differentiation of the musical from other sound events is often not unambiguous, because, historically, sound events structured as ends in themselves frequently develop out of sound productions that have *immediate practical ends*. Thus acoustic signalling languages can be turned into constructions with musical ends in themselves, or the noises of work and working rhythms can lead to the development of work dances and work songs.

2.2 Although the concept of music excludes sound production for exclusively practical ends, it nevertheless includes all those sound effects that serve practical ends and simultaneously display *elements of acoustic ends in themselves*.

2.21 In some cultures there are sound events that are part of the working process, the ritual, war-making, hunting etc., and which nevertheless display elements of ends in themselves (decorative, autonomous, aesthetic elements). The activity directed at the production of these kinds of sound event is here understood as purposeful, its results, however, partly as autonomous (not immediately useful).

2.22 Special terms have been suggested to describe the hybrid status of musical praxis, as it is not dissociated from total social action: e.g. *music embedded in life*[4] or *usage-related music*.[5]

---

4 Walter Wiora, "Die Darbietung lebensgebundener Musik im Rundfunk", in Thomas M. Langer, *Rundfunk und Hausmusik: Gegensatz oder Ergänzung?*, series "Musikalische Zeitfragen" vol. III (Kassel / Basel: 1958), 20-27.
5 Heinrich Besseler, *Das musikalische Hören der Neuzeit* (Berlin: 1959).

Autonomy

3.   At a particular stage of social development a field of the end in itself can develop, i.e. a sphere of human activity that is removed from the socially immediately useful (economic, political) effort: art in the autonomous sense. The emergence of this field, which can be clearly followed in the history of western European music praxis, is a subject of music sociology. This investigates the preconditions, the causes, the history and the consequences of the *autonomisation* of music.

3.1   Autonomisation releases the energies of the aesthetic end in itself that is already contained within life-related, usage-related music (see 2.22). The social change that leads to autonomisation shapes the fate of music: it becomes autonomous art. The precondition for this step to autonomy (see 13.3), however, is also the transition of musical composition into a written form.[6]

Aesthetic Information

4.   With the transition to autonomous art, a change took place in music that information theory[7] had signalled: the transition to the use of sound events to convey information of a primarily aesthetic and not a semantic nature.

4.1   The sound event as a carrier of meaning, i.e. as a carrier of *semantic information,* corresponds to universal logic, is pronounceable and translatable. *Aesthetic information,* however, does not relate to a universal repertoire but to knowledge that is shared by the sender and the recipient; it cannot be translated into another language, because there is no such language.

4.2   In the historical process of the autonomisation of music the aesthetic character becomes ever more pronounced, obviously without completely losing the semantic element.

---

6   Max Weber, *The Rational and Sociological Foundations of Music* (Carbondale: 1958).
7   Abraham A. Moles, *Information Theory and Esthetic Perception* (Champaign: 1966).

Sociology

5.   According to its most general definition as the teaching of human society, sociology should incorporate every social activity within its researches, thus also the artistic.

5.1   Division of labour, which in modern European society has also involved the scientific sphere, brought with it the fact that the description and analysis of individual fields of activity were handed over to the individual disciplines: political science, economics, religious studies, history of art etc.

5.12   Under the compulsion to social division of labour and to the advantage of fundamental detailed analysis, what basically remained profoundly linked within human society was allocated to the individual disciplines.

5.2   In the 19th century this process also led to the establishment of musicology as an independent discipline. Its autonomisation was further promoted by the simultaneous appearance of the tendency to the aesthetic autonomy of music.

5.3   Music sociology again reverses the isolation of musicology in its own field by embedding the subject under investigation into the social reference framework and making the whole of musical praxis the subject of the research, and in this way linking music research to research into society.

Linking the Disciplines

6.   The unification of musicology with sociology can occur in two ways: as a formal connection or as an integration of the content.

6.1   The *formal connection* between musicology and sociology amounts to nothing more than the fact that the methods and understanding of sociology are applied to musicological research. Under this procedure music sociology appears as a form of observation that is still little adapted to the specifics of music. The sociological aspect is simply added to the musicological aspect. This kind of linking of the two sciences represents simply a formal overcoming of the division of labour in academic life.

6.2 The *integration of content* of the two disciplines does not content itself with applying sociological questions to the substrata of musicological research, but endeavours to develop these questions out of the subject itself and/or its musicological analysis. Thus, for example, musicology cannot give any motive for the autonomisation of music (see 3) or for the changing relationship of semantic or aesthetic elements (see 4) without going beyond the strict musicological analysis of the sound event and referring to the changing social behaviour of the individuals and thereby to social change.

7. Music sociology as a science of musical praxis abstains from carrying over prefabricated theories, methods and categories to the object of the research. It rather develops its categories, methods and theories *inherently* out of the object of research.

8. Music sociology comes into its own right where, and only where, the analysis of musical praxis unavoidably demands the analysis of the social behaviour of people and the specific historical structures of human society.

8.1 Regardless of the demand for a research method that is inherent in the subject, music sociology cannot dispense with incorporating the insights developed in general sociology in its analysis, just as it cannot avoid referring to the insights of other individual sciences (of psychology, physiology, acoustics etc.).

8.2 Once the necessity of incorporating the insights of sociology into the research where its object calls for it is understood, the question arises of which of the numerous sociological teaching systems available might support music sociology. A music sociology with a claim to being scientific must resist the temptation to subscribe to one particular system of sociology from the start. It cannot fulfil its task (see 1) if it permits itself to be guided by a pre-formed system of sociology.

8.21 Nevertheless, music sociology must frequently borrow from the existing systems of teachings in general or special sociological categories, methods or theories for its purposes (see 8.1). Music sociology thereby exposes itself to the charge of eclecticism, which it can only refute if it can prove that the borrowing from theories, methods and category tools is appropriate to the object of the investigation as demanded by the principle of inherence (see 7).

8.22 The relationship of music sociology to other theoretical approaches in general or special sociologies that are available is determined by the *degree of usefulness of the contribution* that one or another system of theories may contribute to the solution of specific individual problems of music sociology.

9. What is more, the attempt to estimate the influence of social changes on changes in musical praxis also calls for the investigation of phenomena that are relevant for musical praxis, whose independence of social change is assumed or even just seems possible.

9.1 These include, for example, acoustic perception and its limits, the characteristics of acoustic memory, the relationship of acoustic and optical perception, the physiological foundations of speaking and singing, the formation of tone systems and so on.

9.2 The consideration of music as a societal phenomenon therefore not only includes sociological aspects in the narrow sense, but also touches problems that are dealt with by other particular disciplines: that is, biology, physiology, psychology, acoustics etc.

10. The field of music sociology finally also includes phenomena usually included in the history of ideas, which for their part again are linked to the fundamental facts of social life.

10.1 Thus, for example, it will not be possible to understand music that belongs to particular liturgy without analysing the liturgical norms of the religious community.

10.2 The usual European Middle Ages consideration of the three-part meter as the *tempus perfectum* (as opposed to the two-part *tempus imperfectum*) cannot properly be understood without taking into account the Trinity of Christian theology.

10.3 The sound form of the polychoral musical space of the Renaissance can hardly be explained without reference to the room-acoustic consequences of the architectural style that pre-shapes this sound form.

10.4 The elimination of the harpsichord in the reproduction of 18th century music in the performance practice of the 19th and 20th centuries cannot be adequately appreciated without an analysis of the acoustic characteristic of the new concert halls, of the changes in instrument construction and the related modification of social listening habits.

11. In the course of this analysis the object of music-sociological analysis moves into the fields of those scientific disciplines that facilitate a comprehensive and adequate formulation of questions and answers.

11.1 This working rule, which obliges the individual sciences to cross the boundaries drawn by the division of labour, meant for some sociologists – and not only music sociologists – that they have to face to the accusation that they lack an exact determination of their field, their methods and aims.

11.2 However, music sociology derives its legitimacy precisely from the fact that the established individual sciences cannot cope with numerous objects of research other than their own. Thus, for example, it is impossible to understand the Christian view at the end of antiquity and the early Middle Ages with its complete abandonment of the musical notation developed in antiquity without reference to the economic, juridical and ideological changes of the end of antiquity.

Musical Praxis

12. Music sociology deals with musical praxis (see 1). With this accent on societal-practical action, music sociology distinguishes itself from a primarily philologically oriented musicology, which only rarely goes beyond the consideration of sound events that are recorded or outlined in script symbols.

12.1 The extension of the research field of musicology was already recommended by Guido Adler in 1885, who called for the investigation of the relationship of music to "culture, the climate and national economic circumstances".[8]

---

8 Guido Adler, "Umfang, Methode und Ziel der Musikwissenschaft", *Vierteljahrsschrift für Musikwissenschaft*, 1/1885, 12.

12.2 If one bears in mind that such an attempt must always remain revisable, then the attempted determination of logical historical stages in musical practice following Adler can yield work-related benefits.

13. We describe the logical and historical first stage of the ascertainable behaviour of people in the immediate production of sound events as *musical praxis of the first order*. This stage particularly covers the non-notational production of sound events. The stages of musical practice that use notation only as an aid to memory or as a contribution to providing a norm for musical practice can also for the time being be included in this musical praxis.

13.1 Notation itself is the result of historical development. Even where it strives for it, notation does not achieve the level of the definitive correspondence of written symbols and sound events.

13.2 Certainly notation refers to musical practice, but by no means in an unambiguous way. Within musicology this fact led to the development of a "theory of performance practice". The insights elaborated by this theory form one of the foundations of music sociology in the establishment of what "musical praxis" is.

13.3 Operating with written symbols that stand for sound events itself becomes an element of musical praxis at a particular stage of development (see 3.1). The possibility offered by musical notation to plan and anticipate the completion of sound event (the "performance") through a combination of ("composed") written symbols changes people's relationship to the sound events they conceive and turns them into the advance-planning creator of a self-contained "work" (see 18.2).

13.4 The development of musical notation is one of the preconditions for the emergence of the *composer* in the modern sense. It makes the drafting of musical *works* possible, which to some extent could not even be conceived without the existence of notation.

14. The activity of the composer as *musical praxis of the second order* acquires the character of social activity. It depends upon the technique of musical notation developed by society and it is not without societal consequences: in the written form, the product

of compositional activity has the chance of continued existence, while "non-composed music" can maintain itself only through unbroken passing down, obviously, in a repetition process that is not linked to a binding written form, not being immune to intentional or unintentional reconstructions.

14.1 The following elements, which cannot be verified in the praxis of the first order, are part of the musical praxis of the second order:

14.11 *the activity of the composer*, who draws up a written model to which the production of the sound events has to adhere;

14.12 *the work*, as a model fixed in writing;

14.13 *the interpretation*, i.e. the activity of the person making music, who reads the rules for the production of the sound event from the work.

14.14 These three elements can be considered to be the criteria for distinguishing musical praxis of the second order from praxis of the first order.

Musical Notation and Phonography

15. Musicology has developed methods in order to use the methods of modern musical notation to record in writing manifestations of cultures that only know musical praxis of the first order. Because this musical notation is suited to the patterns of our musical culture, however, it may not be able to represent sound events that diverge from our norms (e.g. intervals that are shorter than the tempered semitone or tone steps that are alien to our musical praxis).

15.1 Present-day musical notation had to be enlarged by additional signs in order to approximate to a written record of sound events from other music cultures. The procedure, however, is questionable, because even qualified specialists often cannot entirely avoid the danger of adapting what they hear to their own listening habits. Since around 1900, in order to counter this problem, comparative musicology (music ethnology) has attempted to develop the most precise possible transcription of sound events into the script.

15.2   Only the introduction of the phonograph offered sufficient basis for the study of music from non-occidental cultures. Through this, the material substrata of the research could be conserved and subject to ever new analytical processes (e.g. with the aid of oscillographs and sonographs. *Phonography* ("sound writing") made the diversion through notation, which was not immune to misinterpretations, unnecessary.

16.   Since about 1900, phonography has also provided a wealth of material to understand performance practice of European-occidental artistic music. The initially mechanical-acoustic, later electro-acoustic recordings of musical acts offered the chance to study practical changes in performance.

17.   Phonographic technology not only brings a *quantitative* increase in the music stockpile of 20th-century culture, but also changes musical praxis *qualitatively* in more than one respect:

17.1   The reproduction of the sound event detached itself temporally from its production by people.

17.2   The electro-acoustic processes enable the production of sound events that would not be achievable in real, immediate sound production by people.

17.3   By storing electro-acoustic impulses that have been created in improvisational freedom or also according to a composition plan (score), the production of sound events can partly or entirely dispense with the usual sound production by music-making and singing people. In such cases the technical realisation of what has been stored replaces the traditional "performance" of the written score.

17.4   The technological recording of sound events permits free availability of the recorded material, which can be compiled ("mounted") in any order and subject to any electro-acoustic manipulation (e.g. frequency-band cutting, reverberation etc.). The end product of the reproduction appears as the result of an *electro-acoustic editing* that is undertaken with a musical intention. This represents a *musical praxis of the third order*.

Historical Stages of Musical Praxis

18.   In all, *three historical stages* of musical praxis can be distinguished:

18.1   Musical praxis of the first order, i.e. the immediate production of sound events by the person using their vocal apparatus and the instruments they have chosen or made.

18.2   Musical praxis of the second order, i.e. the drafting of sound events with the aid of a specially developed musical notation that provides instructions for the realisation of the sound event (composer and work).

18.3   Musical praxis of the third order, i.e. the storing of sound events and/or electronic impulses in electro-acoustic editing with the aim of reproduction that can take place independently of singing or music-making people.

19.   Historically, the development of a musical praxis of a higher order as a rule follows a praxis of a lower order, but different stages can also coexist. It is naturally conceivable that musical praxis of the third order (through records, radio, television) suddenly breaks into a particular culture that only knows musical praxis of the first order (e.g. improvising heterophony without notation). This can actually be observed with the invasion of "western" industrial civilisation in some cultures of Asia and Africa.

19.1   The structuring of historical stages of musical practices does not establish any fixed boundaries. The transitions are fluid.

19.2   One already encounters attempts at notation as an aid to memory in the first stage, even where acoustic tradition and improvisation predominate. Freer improvisation also maintains itself in the second stage, even in the self-contained "work" of the "composer", e.g. as "colouring" of the fixed written vocal line up until the 19th century or as virtuoso "cadence" in concerts for solo instruments and orchestra. The elements of the first stage that are preserved in this way naturally experience some modification under the influence of the praxis of the second stage.

20.   The sense of the division into stages that is proposed here does not consist in pedantically allocating every phenomenon to a

particular stage. The division into stages is simply intended to highlight the three historical stages clearly:

20.1 the immediate relationship of people to the consciously produced sound event in the musical praxis of the first order;

20.2 the mediated relationship to the sound event that is characteristic for the people composing and the people performing the composition (musical praxis of the second order);

20.3 the praxis of electro-acoustic storage and electro-acoustic transformation (editing), freed from the laws of direct sound production ("live" music), the results of which differ qualitatively from the musical praxis of the first and second orders.

Social Facts

21. For the purposes of a sociology of music praxis the concept of *social facts* (differing from *fait social* in Emile Durkheim's sense) is defined as: a situation that has an indirect or direct effect on people's behaviour.

21.1 Here it is irrelevant whether this situation has been brought about by people themselves (property relations, power relations, form of production, technique of production and communication etc.) or whether it represents a "natural" condition of social life (e.g. climatic circumstances):

21.2 the concept of the social fact not only includes *the material and institutional conditions* of human coexistence but also extends to the *intellectual (ideological) circumstances* that affect people's social behaviour: religious or ethical ideas, for example, often have a similarly powerful effect on social behaviour as the material conditions of human coexistence.

21.3 Whether, for its part, the ideological situation is attributable to the material conditions of social life (in the sense of a *materialist understanding of history*) or whether an existence is recognised independent of material conditions (in the sense of an *idealist understanding of history*) remains irrelevant to this stage of the analysis.

21.4 It should, however, be stated that, as a result of their effect on people's social behaviour, ideological circumstances acquire the status of social facts.

21.5 The effect or non-effect of a particular social fact on people's social behaviour can usually only be established if historical development creates conditions that are similar to the repeatable scientific experiment, i.e. where (and then when) in a particular phase of historical development a new social fact appears or a previously existing one ceases to apply.

21.5.1 If a particular human behaviour changes with the appearance of social fact SF_1 or with the disappearance of fact SF_2 in conditions that otherwise remain similar, then a causal relationship between circumstance and behaviour can be presumed.

21.5.2 If, moreover, this change can be shown in the history of different peoples, civilisations etc. then there is an increased probability that the presumed effect on human behaviour can be ascribed to the appearance or disappearance of the social fact.[9]

25. In seeking comparative historical constellations, sociology can draw on the findings and data of historiography, cultural history, art history etc. Comparative musicology (music ethnology) offers particularly rich material for music sociology.

25.1 The examination of this material permits an extension of the analysis to two and more historical constellations and thereby the construction of research approaches that are modelled on the natural science experiment.

25.11 In this way, for example, it can be shown that the conclusion of the circle of fifths, championed by Andreas Werckmeister 1686/87, and the foundation of a tempered scale can of itself in no way be considered to be an SF that was decisive for the change in musical praxis in Europe. The fact that a similar tempering had also been theoretically worked out in China without it having had the consequences for China that we can see in Europe speaks against this.

---

9 Editorial note: the following paragraphs, 22 to 24, have been omitted.

25.2   The penetration of western industrial civilisation into countries such as Japan, on the other hand, shows that there – despite the existence of different tone systems and an artistic music based on them – the European twelve-tone division of the octave can assert itself in musical praxis.

26.   Comparative observations of this kind draw attention to other social facts whose influence on the change in musical praxis may be of importance – thus to the autonomisation of music related to the transition to commodity society and industrial production, which is related to the form of the tone system, which is yet to be determined more closely.

26.1   Music ethnology provides similarly important conclusions in the investigation of the problem of polyphony. The older theory, according to which polyphony developed out of an original monophony, was shattered by the observation of "primitive" types of polyphony.

26.2   The organ music praxis described in European treatises of the Middle Ages (polyphony on the basis of parallel fifths and fourths) also in no way proves to be a construction of the writers of these treatises or as an artificial product, if the observation that such musical practice continued in "retreats" (the Caucasus, Iceland) into the 20th century can be substantiated.[10]

27.   The outline of a stage plan of musical practice attempted here springs from a way of thinking that is linked with the interdisciplinary combination of comparative studies of art and music. It is thus certainly no accident that a music ethnologist whose subject displays a specialist relationship with music sociology already proposed such a pattern half a century ago. Curt Sachs'[11] gradation was:

27.1   Non-noted music: Composer and performer are the same person. The music cannot be disseminated without this person and only has a continued existence in the uncertain form of the tradition.

---

10   Erich M. von Hornbostel, "Phonographierte isländische Zwiegesänge", *Deutsche Islandforschung*, 1/1930; reprinted in id., *Tonart und Ethos: Aufsätze* (Leipzig: 1986).
11   Curt Sachs, *Our Musical Heritage* (New York: 1948), 378.

27.2 Noted music: Separation of the composer from the performer; modest possibilities for the dissemination and continued existence.

27.3 Printed music: Greater possibilities for dissemination and continued existence.

27.4 Technological recording of music (phonography): Complete separation of reproduction from real performance. Unlimited reproduction. Greatest possible chances of dissemination and continued existence in the original form of performance.

Part II
On Max Weber's Sociology of Music

Max Weber and Music Sociology[1]

Max Weber (1864–1920), whom a recognised reference book names as the greatest and most important German sociologist, was a universally educated thinker who made fruitful contributions to the history of law, economic history and the sociology of religion. The diversity of his works probably means that Weber's contributions to the sociology of art and music still have not received the recognition they deserve. Sociologists evidently lacked the knowledge of the scientific categories for music that Weber possessed, and with few exceptions contemporary musicological literature, on the other hand, seldom referred to his music-sociology texts. Thus Tibor Kneif's *Musiksoziologie*[2] devoted only a few lines to possibly the most representative German sociologist, and the name Weber is not mentioned in the index to Peter Rummenhöller's *Einführung in die Musiksoziologie*[3] [Introduction to Music Sociology], while he mentions it at least briefly once in the text.

One of the causes of the neglect of Weber's music sociology can be found in the publishing fate of his work on music sociology, which remained a fragment, published one year after his death, 1921, by Theodor Kroyer and appeared in a second edition in 1924.[4] In his preface he noted that the publisher "had his hands full" with Weber's often indecipherable handwriting. The result presented is far removed from the original text or a critical edition. Astonishingly, the explanation by such an important musicologist as Kroyer claimed that he had altered "only the obviously wrong, otherwise changed nothing" in the text.[5]

Later, Weber's article was not published separately but as an appendix to the more than eleven-hundred pages of the two volume *Wirtschaft und Gesellschaft* [Economy and Society]. Only since 1972 has there again

---

1   Editorial note: first published in *Neue Zürcher Zeitung*, 7./8. July 1979, 61–62.
2   Tibor Kneif, *Musiksoziologie* (Cologne: 1971).
3   Peter Rummenhöller, *Einführung in die Musiksoziologie* (Wilhelmshaven: 1978).
4   Max Weber, *Die rationalen und soziologischen Grundlagen der Musik*, (Munich: 1924). [English: *The Rational and Social Foundations of Music*, translated and edited by D. Martindale, J. Riedel and G. Neuwirth (Carbondale: 1958).]
5   Theodor Kroyer, "Einleitung", in Max Weber, *Die rationalen und soziologischen Grundlagen der Musik*, (Munich: 1924), VIII.

been a separate [German] edition of the work,[6] obviously without the preface by Kroyer, which might enlighten the reader regarding the problem of the form of text. Neither is there any indication that Weber did not intend the text for publication in its present form at all, but that he must have understood it as a working document for seminars and for his own further research. The manuscript apparently has no bibliographic references. The lack of the academic apparatus, however, should not blind us to the fact that Max Weber had prepared for this work with painstaking studies that are characteristic of him. An analysis of the text shows that he was not only thoroughly familiar with works on the psychology of tone since Hermann von Helmholtz and music history writings since Hugo Riemann but also with decisively important contributions on comparative musicology such as the works of Carl Stumpf, Erich Moritz von Hornbostel and others.

A further difficulty to the understanding of the text arises from the fact that it only provides selective information on Weber's understanding of the sociology of art and music. An understanding of the music sociology fragment only discloses itself when one has got to know Weber's thinking on the sociology of arts and music as a whole. These are scattered through his most varied works, above all in those on methodological questions and on the sociology of religion. There has so far been no attempt in the German-speaking world to assess Weber's music sociology fragment within this more comprehensive context of his sociology. The introduction by Don Martindale and Johannes Riedel to the American translation of Weber's work, which appeared in 1958, is an effort to approach this objective.[7]

So much for the obstacles that have so far faced an appreciation of the thinking of Max Weber. It is not the intention of this report systematically to present Weber's ideas on the sociology of music and art, but it should be sufficient to outline some of his ideas, which make it possible to recognise the topicality and fruitfulness of his sociological approaches.

---

6   Max Weber, *Die rationalen und soziologischen Grundlagen der Musik*, series "Uni-Taschenbücher" vol. 122 (Tübingen: 1972). [Editorial note: in the meantime an annotated edition of Weber's sociology of music has been published, see Christoph Braun / Ludwig Finscher (eds.), *Max Weber Gesamtausgabe: Schriften und Reden: Zur Musiksoziologie. Nachlass 1921* (Tübingen: 2004).]
7   Max Weber, *The Rational and Social Foundations of Music*, translated and edited by D. Martindale, J. Riedel and G. Neuwirth (Carbondale: 1958).

Weber placed the establishment of the sociological foundations of music before the discussion of its rational foundation. He raised the question of how various material scales and tone systems were actually historically possible. He answered this question with the mathematical proof that there cannot be a tone system as a "rationally closed entity". In other words, a natural selection of tones from the acoustic continuum that is to be described as correct for musical purposes for all time is inconceivable. This understanding had of course been formulated before Weber, most clearly perhaps by Alexander John Ellis in his essay *On the Musical Scales of Various Nations* (1885), which, however, only became available in German in the translation by Erich Moritz von Hornbostel after Weber's death. At the end of this article it says: "The final conclusion is that the Musical Scale is not one, not natural, not even founded necessarily on the laws of the constitution of musical sound, so beautifully worked out by Helmholtz, but very diverse, very artificial, and very capricious."[8]

Weber goes beyond this finding inasmuch as he progresses to methodological considerations. He distinguishes between *logical correctness* on the one hand and *social validity* on the other. This is not explicitly expounded in his music sociology fragment, however, but in the text of a lecture on methodological problems that Weber gave in 1913 at the Vienna conference of the Association for Social Policy.[9] In this lecture he gave a striking example of the difference between logical correctness and social validity, by pointing out that any description of the existing tone system would have to accept the to our knowledge "wrong" calculation that twelve fifths equals seven octaves.[10]

In the social validity of a particular tone system Weber saw the expression of a maxim of practical musical behaviour, of social action. He defined the concept of social action as the kind of action whose intended meaning relates to the behaviour of others and whose course of action is oriented on that. For him sociology is a science that seeks to understand social action interpretively and through this to explain it causally in its

---

8 Alexander John Ellis, "On the Musical Scales of Various Nations", originally published in *Journal of the Society of Arts*, 33/1885; here quoted from Kay Kaufman Shelemay (ed.), *A Century of Ethnomusicological Thought* (New York: 1990), 527.

9 Max Weber, "The Meaning of 'Ethical Neutrality' in Sociology and Economics", in id., *Max Weber on the Methodology of the Social Sciences*, translated and edited by Edward A. Shils and Henry A. Finch (Glencoe: 1949), 1–47.

10 ibid., 300.

development and its effects. This concept also underlies his music sociology, inasmuch as it undertakes the attempt to trace and explain the historical, cultural and nationally different maxims of musical behaviour.
His primary focus is thus not on the artwork as the crystallised result of
musical action but the process of musical communication in its totality.

The topicality of this approach is easily explained. It becomes clear when
we look at the fate of our current, still valid tone system crystallised in
prefabricated keyboard instruments. In the last 70 years, composition
and composition theory – above all in the field of electronic music – have
not only sought to call the traditional use of this system into question
but through the different selection of tones from the acoustic continuum
have also established a wide range of new systems with the claim at
least to aesthetic validity. For this reason there has been talk of a crisis of
tonality, whatever that may mean, for more than half a century. However, this is faced by the far more spectacular extension of the geographic
area of application of the system developed in Europe, which divides
the octave into twelve equal sections. It is not without dismay that music
ethnologists record this expansion of occidental maxims of musical behaviour into the countries of the Far East, Africa or Latin America.

The often very vehement divergence of the European avant-garde
composers from the traditional norms, which determine the choice of
musical material, thus contrasts with the quantitative and thus socially
significant reception of these norms in wide areas of the Third World.
Here we are dealing with a mass formation of listening habits that
could lead to the mistaken assumption that the efforts of the avant-
garde – precisely because of their limitation to particular circles or regions – might have little prospect of success.

Certainly, technological media have also contributed to the triumph of
music based on the twelve-part division of the octave. Film, television,
radio, records and cassettes not only provide products for consumers
but conversely also have the effect of producing consumers with listening habits that are suited to the products. The extent of a particular, traditional European-occidental maxim of musical behaviour, to use Max
Weber's terminology, is thereby extended to large areas of our planet.

The *laudatores temporis acti* [praisers of past time] derive from this the
conclusion that one must blame this development on the mass media.

Communications research will certainly not support such a thesis, because closer examination shows that, particularly in the audio-visual media in the field of background music, numerous innovations of the avant-garde have been accepted and successfully sold to the public. Thus for example the non-traditional dodecaphonic use of the traditional tone system was already occasionally brought into the Hollywood film studios during the Second World War – and not without success. In the field of background music (in film and television and radio plays) there was and is electronic sound production whose structure frequently contradicts the preferred maxims of the concert hall but which is nevertheless received and accepted without contradiction.

If one applies Weber's teaching of the maxims of social behaviour to this situation then one comes to the conclusion that various maxims of musical behaviour coexist within one society. In other words, it is not permissible to talk of music per se; rather, we are dealing with different musics that hold their own alongside one another, which not only differ from one another with regard to function or intention but also according to the handling of acoustic materials either professed or made available for the particular aims.

Conversely, his turning away from Eurocentric thinking in cultural studies, which Weber demonstrated using the example of the history of the tone system, had the result that he posed the question of the specific developmental conditions of occidental art even more sharply. He explained the possible solution to this problem in various passages in his writing through the attempt to analyse the factual, technical, social and psychological conditions of Gothic architecture. This is not the place to go into this analysis more deeply, but the methodological summary that Weber draws from it is also significant in our context. This summary states: "When the history and sociology of art have uncovered these purely factual technical, social, and psychological conditions of the new style, they have exhausted their purely empirical task."[11]

Weber's research into the world-historic singularity of occidental music follows the same procedure. From the standpoint of the modern European, he describes the central problem as the question: "why did the development of harmonic music from the universally popularly

---

11 Max Weber, "The Meaning of 'Ethical Neutrality' in Sociology and Economics", op. cit., (Glencoe: 1949), 30.

developed folk polyphony take place only in Europe and in a particular epoch, whereas everywhere else the rationalization of music took another and most often quite opposite direction."[12]

Weber recognised the most important sociological factor in this context because of his comprehensive studies of the sociology of religion in the formation of monasticism in the northern-occidental missionary area, a monasticism which – as he mentions elsewhere – transformed asceticism into a specific occupational service within the church.

Music within the church was to fulfil a rationally conceived, disciplining function. One main feature of this disciplining of people consisted, with serious consequences, in the detachment of linguistic-musical communication from physical movement, in the desensualisation of music. This disembodiment of music had serious consequences for the further development of music. Weber himself did not use the expression *disembodiment*, but this term, which we have chosen, precisely corresponds to the pull towards desensualisation that Weber describes in his religious sociological explanations of monasticism. The call for desensualised, disembodied devotion to the liturgy is already pithily described in Augustine's *Confessions*, and is repeatedly raised in writings of the Early Middle Ages, most clearly perhaps by Smaragdus Abbas Virdunensis in his *Commentary on the Rule of Saint Benedict*: "opportet psallentem immobili corpore, inclinato capite stare, et laudes Domino moderate canere." ["The person singing should stand with motionless body and bowed head, and sing praises to the Lord with composure."][13]

In his writings Weber did not explicitly mention the exclusion of gesture, movement and dance from the Christian liturgy, but the important consequences of this disembodiment of song can be inferred from many of his explanations. Added to this is the fact that his pupil Paul Honigsheim reports a discussion with Weber in which he referred to the particular significance of the animosity to dance in the Christian liturgy.[14]

---

12 ibid., 30.
13 Smaragdus of Saint Mihiel, *Commentary on the Rule of Saint Benedict*, trans. David Barry, Cistercian Studies, No. 212 (Kalamazoo: 2007), 333. [Blaukopf quoted from Franz Müller-Heuser: *Vox humana: Ein Beitrag zur Untersuchung der Stimmästhetik des Mittelalters*. (Regensburg: 1963), 163, footnote 89.]
14 Paul Honigsheim, "Erinnerungen an Max Weber", *Kölner Zeitschrift für Soziologie und Sozialpsychologie*, yr. 15, special issue vol. 7, 1963, 248.

This disembodiment as a maxim of musical action is an essential precondition for a specific feature of occidental musical development. With this, for the first time the detachment of the musical from the gestural on the one hand and from dance on the other was initiated. With the spread of musical notation, the emergence of composers and the assumption of the print accent from dance rhythm, the later special development that Weber described as the "father of the music forms that led to the sonata" built upon this. Consequently, this release of the musical process from the involvement of the body and the development of music ultimately as an autonomous art is just as little a natural process as the development of the tone system that was to serve occidental artistic music. In Weber's music sociology, all these evolutions appear as results of the assertion of particular maxims of musical behaviour, which are shaped by factual, technical, sociological and psychological conditions.

By drawing attention to the ideal-type development tendency of the separation of music and bodily movement, Weber not only deepens the understanding of a specific contribution of monasticism and its historical consequences, but also paves the way to dealing with current music sociology problems, even to the understanding of questions of music teaching. Music pedagogics is only too familiar with the difficult problems that arise when learning how to deal with music is largely divorced from the synaesthetic, motor and autonomic context. New research in the area of music therapy even justifies the view that such a separation of the purely musical has an artificial nature. Without doubt, we owe sublime works of art, whose value for us is unquestioned, to this separation. But this does not alter the fact that something unnatural in the true sense of the word is attached to the separation of the musical from physical participation.

Even more: the outbreak of physically vital music behaviour is evidently to be understood as a rejection of this separation of absolute music as art, as a thoroughly natural expression of life. Occasionally such a rejection assumes an epidemic character: in the dance mania of the 14th century, in the waltz fever of the 19th century, in the Dixieland and jazz wave that flooded over Europe after the First World War, or also in the rock, beat and pop movement that broke out in the 1960s.

The topicality of Max Weber's music sociology proves itself precisely in the analysis of such a current phenomenon. His sociology does not exhaust itself in seeking to discover the reflection of the economic bone structure of society in musical phenomena. He is not content with much loved and questionable theses in fashionable sociology today about the imprinting of power relations in the structure of musical works. He abstains from stating that analogy between politics and art is sociology, but he concretely analyses the conditions that lead to the genesis of a particular socio-musical behaviour.

Nowhere in Weber's statements on the sociology of music and art does he claim to be replacing aesthetics and musicology by sociology. What he strives for is *to make a contribution to cultural studies from the point of view of sociology and with the categories of sociological thought*. His methodological approach is therefore also not far removed from that formulated by Guido Adler in his inaugural academic address at the University of Vienna on 26 October 1898: "Music forms part . . . of the total field of intellectual productions and like all these proves to be dependent on social, economic, political conditions of all kinds. In the way that the actual specialist area of our music-historical research is handled with great success, the new task of rolling up all these connecting threads opens up for future generations."[15]

Rolling up connecting threads is also the task that Weber sets for music sociology. It is not his intention to superimpose a sociological category system on musicology but to trace the concrete conditions of change in the maxims of musical behaviour and to contribute the inventory of these conditions to musicology. Alongside the preconditions that Adler mentions – namely the *social, economic* and *political* – Weber also insists on the *technical* conditions of art and music. In these one can see an aspect that is particularly topical in the age of technological media.

Weber sees the main task in the analysis of the progress of the technical means of art or also of the external technical preconditions of art. He freely admits that a valuing consideration of art is not possible without the concept of progress, but he believes that the empirical history of art must operate without such a concept. In contrast, however, it is precisely properly understood *technical* progress that is "the domain of art history", because the analysis of the influence of the technical on the *Kunstwollen*[16] makes it possible to show what is ascertainable in

---

15 Guido Adler, "Musik und Musikwissenschaft", *Jahrbuch der Musikbibliothek Peters für 1898* (Leipzig: 1899), 35.

16 Editorial note: *Kunstwollen* can be literally translated as "the will to art" but its

the course of art and music history without a value judgement.[17] He gives examples of this in more or less detailed ways: such as the role of iron production in the manufacture of the modern piano, which for its part again opened up competition between piano factories and led instrument makers to build their own concert halls. As Weber put it, this was "finally analogous to salesman techniques of breweries".[18] The example shows how technologically, economically and ultimately also performance practice and stylistic aspects are interwoven.

Nor did Weber omit to point out that the acoustic characteristic of the music room can be a technologically determining factor. Thus in the 1917 revised version of the above-mentioned Vienna lecture of 1913, he says: "Finally the development of the piano-forte – one of the most important technical instruments of modern musical development – and its dissemination in the bourgeois class, was rooted in the specific character of the rooms in the buildings in the North European culture area."[19]

Weber's admittedly sparse remarks on the music room once again draw attention to the importance of the room for the musical structure itself, which can be read from the writings of the 18th century, for the terms theatre style, church style and chamber style, which should not only be understood as style categories but also as technological characterisations that arise from different lengths of reverberation times. Thereby

---

actual meaning has nothing common with a voluntaristic theory. *Kunstwollen* refers to the idea that in some cases a shared intentional framework, or to put it differently, a historically contingent tendency of an age towards a particular artistic and stylistic development can be observed. This idea applies not only to the individual artists and artworks but also to the general public. Then *Kunstwollen* denotes a predominant way of aesthetic perception and a common form of artistic imagination in a particular age and society. Alois Riegl does not deduce *Kunstwollen* from an idealistic-speculative theory like Hegel's philosophy of history, rather he aims to elaborate it through inductive, empirical and comparative analysis. See also Blaukopf's text "The Sociological Concept of the Kunstwollen and its origins in the Austrian School of Art History and Musicology", in this anthology, page 95–107.

17 Max Weber, "The Meaning of 'Ethical Neutrality' in Sociology and Economics", op. cit., (Glencoe: 1949), 1–47.

18 Max Weber, *The Rational and Social Foundations of Music*, op. cit., (Carbondale: 1958), 122.

19 Max Weber, "The Meaning of 'Ethical Neutrality' in Sociology and Economics", op. cit., (Glencoe: 1949), 31-32.

Weber – we cannot say whether consciously or not – was picking up observations by Quantz, Forkel and E. T. A. Hofmann – observations that were also present in Stendhal, in the notes on his Rossini biography, or in Berlioz in the composition of some works and in some of his essays. The topicality of such considerations is not only confirmed by the works of Heinrich Besseler[20] but also by research into concert-hall acoustics such as that carried out by Fritz Winckel.[21]

Weber's insistence on the technical conditions of musical communication as the key to understanding different maxims of musical behaviour is particularly striking because he died four years before the beginning of the spread of the European radio network, and he could certainly hardly know anything of the triumphal march of electro-acoustic recording and reproduction of music as we know it today. He was only familiar with the primitive methods of mechanical, non-electrical recording of music, which had been used by music ethnologists and phonogram archives since the start of the century. Weber recognised the importance of this method, writing: "Only recently has empirical knowledge available through phonograms of primitive music supplied materials for a more adequate picture of origins."[22]

In the light of the development of music recording, music reproduction and the electronic synthesis of composition in the last three decades, Max Weber's call for an examination of the influence of technology on *Musikwollen* [the will to music] seems particularly topical. Thus – just to mention one example – the storage of acoustic signals has created the possibility of making the reproduction of the musical message largely independent of the acoustic characteristics of the performance room itself. The interposing of echo chambers or reverberation devices opens the possibility of creating artificial acoustic spaces. Multi-channel technology can go a step further by providing signals from various sources with different reverberation times. The effect that these and similar processes of studio techniques can have on listening behaviour, listening habits and listener expectations have hardly been researched

---

20 Heinrich Besseler, "Musik und Raum", in id. (ed.), *Festschrift für Max Seiffert* (Kassel: 1938).

21 Fritz Winckel, "Akustik im festlichen Haus", *Bauwelt*, yr. 48, 51/1957; id., *Phänomene des musikalischen Hörens* (Berlin: 1960).

22 Max Weber, *The Rational and Social Foundations of Music*, op. cit., (Carbondale: 1958), 33.

yet. Weber's music-sociological studies implicitly, and in some places in his writings explicitly, point out the necessity of such analyses, which could presumably contribute to the understanding of the mutation process that present-day musical communication is subject to.

Apart from such topical aspects, which have here been supported by a few examples, Weber's music sociology contains some further methodological elements that can be of use to historical research. His sociology does not content itself with the establishment of facts, nor with the interpretation and explanation of social activity. He ascribes an essential critical task to science: also to call what is taken for granted into question. "The specific function of science, it seems to me . . . namely to ask questions about these things which convention makes self-evident."[23]

It is also a question of this ethos when talking about the topicality of Max Weber.

---

23 Max Weber, "The Meaning of 'Ethical Neutrality' in Sociology and Economics", op. cit., (Glencoe: 1949), 33.

The Concept of Progress in Music Sociology[1]

If one tends to assume that "ways to a formulated theory of progress in music are in principle possible",[2] then it is recommendable to examine the aspects in music where it is possible to talk of progress. Music sociology poses itself this question. It distinguishes at least three such aspects:

a) progress in artistic development itself;
b) progress in the development and use of the technical means employed for the creation and dissemination of music;
c) progress in the realisation of the democratic policy demand to facilitate participation in music culture and access to music culture for the greatest possible number of people.

Each of these questions deserves to be treated separately.

Progress in Artistic Development

For a long time a Eurocentric view led to modern occidental music being regarded as the "highest". There are still traces of this way of thinking in Hermann Kretzschmar. Hegel had already expressed fundamental reservations about it. In reference to older works of fine art, which to modern aesthetic awareness appeared imperfect or clumsy, Hegel said that their creation would just have corresponded to a different aesthetic consciousness. What seemed imperfect to later observers was "not unintentional technical inexpertness and incapacity, but conscious alteration, which depends upon the content that is in consciousness, and is, in fact, demanded by it".[3]

This understanding of a respectively specific aesthetic consciousness established itself in the Vienna School of Art History, although without reference to Hegel. Alois Riegl (1858-1905) saw the art work as the result of a particular deliberate *Kunstwollen*. The category of *Kunstwollen*

---

1 Editorial note: first published in Hanns-Werner Heister (ed.), *Musik/Gesellschaft: Zwischen Erklärung & Kulturindustrie: Festschrift für Georg Knepler zum 85. Geburtstag* (Hamburg: 1993), 21–30.
2 Georg Knepler, *Geschichte als Weg zum Musikverständnis: Zur Theorie, Methode und Geschichte der Musikgeschichtsschreibung* (Leipzig 1977), 531.
3 Georg W. F. Hegel, "Vorlesungen über die Ästhetik", in id., *Werke*, vol. 13 (Frankfurt: 1970), 106.

became a central one in art sociology. Occasionally, reservations have been voiced against this term: it may have a mystic character and leads to explaining artistic achievement as being based on a preconceived, speculative principle. Against this, the Riegl pupil Hans Tietze objected that with *Kunstwollen* it was "not about a special mystical power, about an urge of a people . . . but about a term that has solely been gained from the works and other expressions, which serves for the orientation of all new additional individual objects but which can also experience further extension and modification".[4]

This concept is inseparably connected with the rejection of the idea of an absolute and eternally valid highest aesthetic ideal. The philosophical construction of absolute beauty has been taken so far that one seeks "laws" that are supposed to be valid for all branches of art. This conception was already rejected by Franz Grillparzer, and Eduard Hanslick even argued emphatically against it: "The servile dependence of the various special aesthetics upon a supreme metaphysical principle of a general aesthetics is steadily yielding ground to the conviction that each particular art demands to be understood only of itself, through a knowledge of its unique technical characteristics. System-building is giving way to research firmly based on the axiom that the laws of beauty proper to each particular art are inseparable from the distinctive characteristics of its material and its technique."[5]

This empirical approach, which was later to become determining for music sociology, was also held in the field of Austrian ethnology. Thus Michael Haberlandt subscribed to the view that the concept of beauty could not be acquired deductively but had to be derived from people's respective behaviour.[6] This way of thinking is also characteristic of Guido Adler. He speaks of the "research of the laws of art of diverse periods"[7]

---

4   Hans Tietze, *Die Methode der Kunstgeschichte* (Leipzig: 1913), 14.
5   Eduard Hanslick, *On the Musically Beautiful: A Contribution toward the Revision of the Aesthetics of Music*, translated and edited by Geffrey Payzant (Indianapolis: 1986), 2.
6   Michael Haberlandt, *Die Welt als Schönheit: Gedanken zu einer biologischen Ästhetik* (Vienna: 1905), 4.
7   Guido Adler, "Methode der Musikgeschichte", op.cit., quoted from Erica Mugglestone, "Guido Adler's 'The Scope, Method, and Aim of Musicology': An English Translation with an Historico-Analytical Commentary", *Yearbook for Traditional Music*, vol. 13 (1981), 16.

and he denies the existence of occidental criteria of artistic beauty.[8] Quite in the spirit of Tietze Adler seeks to discover the guiding "ideal of the will" [*Willensideal*] behind artistic creation[9] and he subscribes to the concept of the *Kunstwollen* that is not philosophically deduced but empirically apprehended: "It is more important to establish what emerges from the art work as creative intent than to attempt to construct the *Kunstwollen* in the abstract."[10]

Common to the considerations of the Rieglian school of art history and of Adlerian musicology is the fact that they do not ascribe any scale to the empirically establishable manifestations of *Kunstwollen* and that this understanding of "higher" or "lower" *Kunstwollen* in a general sense cannot be spoken of. This accords just as much with the concepts of music ethnology as with those of music sociology. The application of the term progress to forms of *Kunstwollen* is therefore not possible, even if it should be noted that "progress" may very well be noticeable in individual cases in relation to particular aspects of artistic creation. Thus, for example, a particular *Kunstwollen* may be linked to the respective function of musical creation – to such an extent that one and the same composer registers so to say two kinds of *Kunstwollen*. This is true for example of the creative intention that Haydn associated with the symphony on the one hand and the string quartet on the other. The structure of Haydn's music "for listeners" differs from the "music for players", which wrenched itself away from the Baroque tradition more quickly.[11]

The Progress of Technical Means

Both music history and music sociology research have recently paid greater attention to the significance of the technical means of musical creation and musical communication. This has led to a more thorough knowledge of the role of technical innovations, which facilitate, promote and even determine the "mutations" of musical communication.[12] The mutation of musical life induced by electronic media has

---

8   Guido Adler, "Methode der Musikgeschichte", op. cit., 121.

9   ibid., 12.

10   ibid., 10.

11   cf. Reginald Barreh-Ayres, *Joseph Haydn and the String Quartet* (London: 1974), 71f.

12   Kurt Blaukopf, *Musik im Wandel der Gesellschaft* (Munich: 1982).

been called "mediamorphosis".[13] In contrast, Smudits[14] described each technical transformation of cultural communication as mediamorphosis and distinguished the following historical stages of mediamorphosis: "the 'written', which is associated with the invention of writing, the 'graphic', which can be marked with the invention of printing, the 'chemical-mechanical', characterised by photography and the gramophone and later through film, the 'electronic', characterised by tone and/or image recording and/or transmission, and the 'digital', which started with the invention of the computer."[15]

The theory of mediamorphosis threw the light on the importance of musical notation for music, which Max Weber had already emphasised and whose relatively limited regard in traditional musical historiography is rightly regretted.[16]

There is some readiness to interpret the elevation of music to written form as progress. Music sociology considerations object to this for the good reason that the notation also implies losses. Notation acts as a kind of filter, by noting some characteristics of the sound and disregarding others as being secondary for the music.[17] Just the difficulties that music ethnologists experience with the "transcription" of non-European musics indicate that these musics contain elements that will definitely be lost in music that is noted in the occidental system.

It is certainly very true that without musical notation the progress towards to some extent complex scores would not have been possible; at the same time, however, this evolution also entailed losses, as elements that could not be noted had to be sacrificed. A win-loss calculation takes place in the field of rhythm, too, if for example we consider

---

13 Kurt Blaukopf, *Beethovens Erben in der Mediamorphose: Kultur- und Medienpolitik für die elektronische Ära.* (Heiden: 1989). [Editorial note: see also Blaukopf's text "The Mediamorphosis of Music as Global Phenomenon" in this anthology, p. 63–89.]

14 Alfred Smudits, *Kommunikationstechnologien und Kunst: Mediamorphosen des Kulturschaffens,* Habilitation (Vienna: 1990) [editorial note: published as *Mediamorphosen des Kulturschaffens: Kunst und Kommunikationstechnologien im Wandel* (Vienna: 2002)].

15 ibid., 46.

16 For instance Georg Knepler, *Geschichte als Weg zum Musikverständnis: Zur Theorie, Methode und Geschichte der Musikgeschichtsschreibung* (Leipzig: 1977), 205.

17 cf. Trevor Wishart, "Musical Writing, Musical Speaking", in John Shepherd et al., *Whose Music: A Sociology of Musical Languages* (London: 1977), 135.

the rhythmic diversity of some non-European musics (e.g. the Indian) and compare them with the standardised period structure of occidental music, which forms a precondition for the modern ways of making and listening to music that Heinrich Besseler[18] analysed.

The transformation of music into a written form is inherently linked with the standardisation of the equally tempered twelve-step tone system. Here, too, losses should be noted. The transition from a multiple "mid-tone" tuning to the norm of equal tempering certainly extended the possibilities of modulation (and in this respect represents progress), but this achievement was paid for by the loss of the differentiation of the character of the various kinds of tone that could previously be felt.[19]

Similar considerations also hold true for the change in instruments. The introduction of the valve horn can be regarded as an advance, but we should not partly or even wholly disregard the abandonment of the unique sound character of the "stuffed" tones of the horn. In all, it can be said that progress in the development of the technical means of music is definitely noticeable in individual cases and that at the same time "production costs" appear, which, following Hanns Eisler, Knepler discusses.[20]

This limited application of the concept of progress to the material and technological preconditions of music is opposed by a radically different one that equates the progress of the "material" with the progress of music itself: "It is not its individual works but its material that provides the scene of progress in art."[21] A composer and theoretician whose importance for music-sociological thinking has previously been too little valued came out against this thesis. We mean Ernst Krenek, who – very much in line with Alois Riegl – came out against such an understanding of progress in music: "If (however) the degree of progressiveness of an achievement is to be seen in its conscious insertion in the respective historical state of the musical material, then this little ghostly independent life of the material will first have to be proven."[22]

---

18 Heinrich Besseler, *Das musikalische Hören der Neuzeit* (Berlin: 1959).
19 Arthur H. Benade, *Fundamentals of Musical Acoustics* (New York: 1976), 312.
20 Georg Knepler, *Geschichte als Weg zum Musikverständnis: Zur Theorie, Methode und Geschichte der Musikgeschichtsschreibung* (Leipzig: 1977), 533.
21 Theodor W. Adorno, "Reaktion und Fortschritt", *Anbruch*, yr. 12, 1930, 191.
22 Ernst Krenek, "Fortschritt und Reaktion", *Anbruch*, yr. 12, 1930, 196.

Nor does the concept of mediamorphosis in any way accord the material-technological preconditions of music the role of a measure on which the progress of *Kunstwollen* can be read. The findings on the metamorphosis of music show only the possibilities just as much as the boundaries of the realisation of a particular will [*Wollen*]. Thus equal tempering opened up new possibilities: the fact that it was used depended on the *Kunstwollen*. It was similar with the perspective technique in fine art. In its complete form it was not developed by painters but by architects. The fact, however, that the *Kunstwollen* of the painters strove for perspective is shown by numerous artists' attempts to achieve a single vanishing point in their pictures.

The kind of approach process that was borne by the *Kunstwollen* can also be agnosticised in the progress to equal temperature. Only "non-musicians"[23] had the mathematical knowledge necessary to outline the tempering. The use of the results was dependent on the decision of the musician.

This interaction of technical knowledge and technical means on the one hand and artistic intent on the other is also characteristic of music creation in the 20th century: the technological potential of electronic sound synthesis was not created by the musicians but by oscillation researchers. The musicians decide whether and how this potential is used. Social division of labour and specialisation have broken the earlier close connections between technology and the creation of art. For this reason, the historical perspectives of a mediamorphosis that they have experienced are not immediately clear to the artists. Only technological and sociological reflection opens such a perspective. An early and illustrious example of this is Ernst Krenek's prognosis in 1938: "The reproduction of the work of music from the record or a similar sound source could become a first-class reproduction as soon as the technological conditions allow the composer to record his work directly, i.e. technologically . . . without the use of music paper. In this case, the script and the sound of the work would be identical, its original – today represented in the score – would coincide with the means of reproduction and the whole complex of the interpretation of a work of music would completely disappear."[24]

---

23 Mark Lindley, "Stimmung und Temperatur", in Frieder Zaminer (ed.), *Hören, Messen und Rechnen in der frühen Neuzeit*, series "Geschichte der Musiktheorie" vol. 6 (Darmstadt: 1987), 328.

24 Ernst Krenek, "Bemerkungen zur Rundfunkmusik", *Zeitschrift für Sozialforschung*, vol. VII, 1938; quoted from Oskar Negt (ed.), *Kritische Kommunikationsforschung* (Munich: 1973), 65.

As far as I can see, this is the earliest indication of the possible consequences of mediamorphosis for composing. These consequences have
in the meantime become the object of systematic research that seeks to
calculate the gains and losses of technological innovations.[25]

Progress in the Realisation of Democratic Policy Maxims

One can also talk of progress if the democratic demand that says the
greatest number of citizens should be afforded access to music and participation in musical culture is to be met. In the democratic-political
sense, only such an extension of the "social reach"[26] [i.e. of public access to culture] could be regarded as progress. Some activities of choir
associations in the 19th century may be regarded as self-help measures
[in sense of self-empowerment] of predominantly bourgeois strata.
The "Workers' Symphony Concerts" set up in Vienna at the start of
the 20th century (of which to my knowledge there were no significant
parallels elsewhere) were of similar importance for the working class.
The democratic demand on which such enterprises base themselves
was also taken account of in sociology at the beginning of our century
– although only occasionally. Thus a participant in the German Sociology Conference of 1910 stated: "Using scientific research to find a way
to provide the masses with greater access to modern cultural goods, to
distribute them to them more, to minimise their hoarding on the one
hand and to distribute them equally on the other, would in my view
be a problem in the issue of culture and technology that would be well
worth the effort of the nobility."[27]

Recently, not only cultural sociology but also cultural policy has shown
clear attempts to cope with this problem. A powerful impulse for this
was the Unesco Intergovernmental Conference on Institutional, Ad-
ministrative, and Financial Aspects of Cultural Policy (Venice 1970)
and the conference on cultural policy in Europe (Helsinki 1972). These

---

25 cf. Kurt Blaukopf: *Beethovens Erben in der Mediamorphose: Kultur- und Medienpolitik
    für die elektronische Ära* (Heiden: 1989); Jon Frederickson, "Technology and Music
    Performance in the Age of Mechanical Reproduction", *International Review of the
    Aesthetics and Sociology of Music*, vol. 20, no. 2, 1989.
26 Georg Knepler, *Geschichte als Weg zum Musikverständnis: Zur Theorie, Methode
    und Geschichte der Musikgeschichtsschreibung* (Leipzig: 1977), 521.
27 Deutsche Gesellschaft für Soziologie (ed.), *Verhandlungen des Ersten Deutschen
    Soziologentages vom 19.-22. Oktober 1910* (Tübingen: 1911), 94f.

triggered national initiatives that were guided by democratic values and pursued the following aims:

a) the democratisation of culture, i.e. the improvement of access to culture and the participation of the whole population in cultural life, and

b) the improvement of the situation of artists, which is the object of a recommendation agreed by the Unesco General Conference in 1980.

The first of the objectives mentioned here is identical with the programme to extend the "social reach". There seems to be a noticeably broad international consensus that the democratisation of music culture is desirable and that the success of such endeavours for democratisation can be regarded as advance.

The majority of the many researches carried out in the 1980s – they are so numerous that they cannot be listed here – came to the conclusion that access to culture and participation in cultural life cannot result from the market-economy interplay of supply and demand. This was, for example, expressed in a study of music policy and the music industry that was carried out in Belgium and which is of exemplary significance for other countries too, and above all for small states.[28] Its author may have concentrated on the role of the music industry and its relationship to the institutions of musical life, but he was not content with an analysis of the situation but also identified elements of a music policy that could have advantageous effects on cultural life through the correction of economic conditions.[29] According to this, progress in the democratic sense is inseparably linked to the readiness to intervene in the music market. From this comes the call for market corrections[30] and the concept of a "cultural market economy",[31] which envisages the correction of the free play of supply and demand.

---

28 André Lange, *Stratégies de la musique* (Brussels: 1986).

29 Robert Wangermée, "Préface", in André Lange, *Stratégies de la musique* (Brussels: 1986), 9.

30 Erika Wahl-Zieger, *Theater und Orchester zwischen Marktkräften und Marktkorrektur: Existenzprobleme und Überlebenschancen eines Sektors aus wirtschaftstheoretischer Sicht* (Göttingen: 1978).

31 Kurt Blaukopf, *Beethovens Erben in der Mediamorphose: Kultur- und Medienpolitik für die elektronische Ära* (Heiden: 1989).

Under the conditions of the present mediamorphosis of music, which is marked by the industrial production of music goods, by the central role of the radio companies as providers of music and by the cable and satellite systems, such a strategy is of decisive importance. The increasing impact of commercial radio companies is likely to bring about conditions that narrow the "social reach" of important parts of our musical culture. The programme strategy of the commercial companies brings with it a situation in musical life that can be described in the following words: "Culture is becoming a well fenced-off domain, and one takes care that the uninitiated are kept from straying into it."[32]

Under these conditions, democratic progress in the field of music proves to be dependent on "market corrections", which can assume various forms (and to some extent already have done). These include:

a) statutory music policy, i.e. political programme tasks that the radio companies have to obey in the cultural interest (such as those laid down for the statutory public broadcasters in some countries);

b) regulations providing that private radio companies are to use an appropriate part of their advertising income for culturally significant purposes themselves or to make it available for this (which has been attempted in the approach of British media legislation).

Summary

For the reasons explained here, in music sociology it is very much a question of progress if it concerns the realisation of the principle of the greatest "social reach" of music. Some elements of such progress can be apprehended and even measured through empirical surveys. The basis is thereby created not only for taking stock of musical life but also for an evaluation of measures intended to serve democratic policy objectives, such as measures to expand the audience for performance music, for decentralising musical institutions and activities and to promote professional music creation. These kinds of evaluation of national music policies have been carried out in some countries.[33]

32 Gabriel Thoveron, "Grande musique – haute culture – petit écran", in Henri Vanhulst / Malou Haine (eds.), *Musique et Société Hommage à Robert Wangermée* (Brussels: 1988), 270.

33 cf. Council of Europe (Conseil de l'Europe), *La politique culturelle de la France* (Paris: 1988); Council of Europe, *Swedish State Cultural Policy: Objectives,*

In relation to the evolution of the technical means of music (from the instruments to tone systems and notation systems to the latest technological innovations) music sociology seeks to estimate the individual elements and calculates both "gains" and "losses".

Music sociology endeavours to record historical stages of the *Kunstwollen* analytically and to compare them in their ideal types. There seem to be weighty reservations against the application of the term "progress" to such changes, because such a procedure could mislead us into seeing the *Musikwollen* [will to music] of a particular culture as "retarded" in comparison to the will to music in another culture. Previous experience with these kinds of understanding – above all the Eurocentric – seems to justify this reservation.

Measures and Results (Stockholm: 1990); IRMO (Institut za razvoj i medunarodne odnose), *La politique culturelle en Yougoslavie – son évaluation et sa comparaison a vec trois pays en développement structure fédérale* (Zagreb: 1989).

Part III
Mediamorphosis

The Mediamorphosis of Music as Global Phenomenon[1]

The reflections contained in this book have been limited – with the exception of several digressions used for purposes of comparison – to Occidental cultures. But the sociology of music cannot remain within these borders, because its concept of intercultural comparison requires that the sociology of music be extended to those cultures that have so far been relegated primarily to ethnomusicology. The convergence of music sociology and ethno-musicology thus seems to be necessary: "Whether they merge or not, an effort should certainly be made by music sociologists and ethnomusicologists to keep better informed about each others' work" (Sorce Keller 1986, 179).

The increasing interdependence of our planet's cultures also challenges both disciplines to cooperate. Given the hitherto limited intercultural communication, it was impossible to speak of a "world history of music." Thus, until recently, it may have been sufficient to view individual musical cultures in their (relative) isolation. The present mutation has made global coherence a central theme of research. Whereas there has until recently been no universal history of music, one has now been created with the mutation induced by the electronic media.

It seems appropriate to explain the particular characteristics of this global mutation, which has no parallel among the historic mutations known to date. A prominent feature of this metamorphosis (although not its only aspect) is the dominant role of the electronic media. In order to visualize this specific aspect, I call the present mutation the mediamorphosis of music.

Features of Mediamorphosis

The concept of mediamorphosis that I have proposed (Blaukopf 1989) seeks to do justice to the real interconnections of all factors currently influencing music, and at the same time to bring out the particular elements of this present mutation. These elements include

---

1 Editorial note: first published in *Musical Life in a Changing Society: Aspects of Music Sociology* (Portland: 1992), 247–270; translation by David Marinelli.

1. The quantitative, therefore economic, dominance of music played by the electronic media. One result of this preponderance of electronically reproduced music is that the effectiveness of measures taken to promote "live" music is reduced.
2. The mediamorphosis of the idea of copyright. For example, the income from the media use of copyrighted music cannot always be unequivocally assigned to individual authors, which leads to a "collectivization" of claims. A striking example of this is the distribution of earnings from the tax many countries impose on blank audio cassettes. The income from these taxes may be divided among authors or even be used for general social or cultural purposes.
3. The loss of the perception that music has a unique aura. "Live music" has an event character that is lacking in the omnipresent media music because of its reproducibility. Mediamorphosis creates what French sociologists have called the "banalization" of music.
4. The separation of music dissemination from performance practice. The sounds that reach the consumer's senses through the loudspeaker have not always been performed as perceived by the consumer.
5. The infiltration of technology not only into the dissemination of music but also into the creative process. All types of popular music have long since ceased to exist primarily as symbols a composer sets to paper or in the form of traditional music-making but have become electronically formed sound.
6. The use of the new technological apparatus for "applied media music." This use of technology also satisfies the demand of radio broadcast companies and the advertising industry for such things as commercial spots, jingles, signature tunes, and background music.
7. The increasing influence of mediamorphosis on the creation of "serious music." The composer who works at his desk now is joined by the creator of music who works in a studio with tools that include sound synthesis, computer programs, and sampling. Ernst Krenek predicted this change in the composer's working method as long ago as 1938.

Several of the consequences of mediamorphosis have been treated in the literature. Jon Frederickson has written an instructive survey summarizing the results of recent research and commenting on his own observations. He emphasizes the crucial innovation – that technology "can create a simulated musical world without performers"

(Frederickson 1989, 197). Moreover, he derives other aspects of contemporary musical life from this change: the expectations of the listening public are increasingly influenced by recording techniques, so "live music" tries to emulate the sound of music conveyed by technical means (ibid., 199); in music conveyed by technical means the aura of intimacy created by "live music" is replaced by greater volume (ibid., 200); the recording engineer becomes of crucial importance in ensemble music conveyed by technical means (ibid., 201); the technology that makes possible the use and transformation of individual musical performances creates copyright questions for which there are as yet no legal provisions (ibid., 202); the direct communication of musical performers characteristic of live music can be replaced by "computerized manipulation of sounds" (ibid., 204); and technology divorces music from the spatial experience associated with it, thereby changing the perception of acoustical architecture (ibid., 205).

These statements, which I have outlined here only in part, indicate the immediately practical changes resulting from the availability of new technologies. Several general tendencies of mediamorphosis emerge that are present in both industrialized and developing countries.

The global importance of these changes reinforces the previously mentioned convergence of sociological and ethnological research provoked by the mediamorphosis of music. Thus, for example, the concepts of "westernization" and "modernization," as used by ethnomusicology (e.g., Nettl 1985), are also of growing importance to sociological research.

In order to understand westernization and modernization it is absolutely essential to abandon the idea of a predetermined international order, an imperative evolution, as it were, from "lower" to "higher." The notion of such an order is based on biological, anthropological, and socioeconomic ideas that must be examined by music sociology because they play a role in the sociological constructions of many thinkers and because, in my opinion, they tend to hinder the value-free evaluation of facts.

Simplifying systems, which may have been of help in popularizing the theories of Charles Darwin, can in fact mislead one to interpret "development" as a process that must lead from a "lower stage" to a "higher stage." The words "evolution" and "progress" alone heavily suggest this interpretation. Modern biology, however, shows that organisms can just as easily go down as up each rung of the evolutionary ladder, which also means, for example, from the organic to the inorganic (cf. Lorenz 1978, 27). Anthropology suggests similar considerations, contending that the progress of the human race cannot be compared to a person climbing steps (cf. Lévi-Strauss 1975, 109). Socioeconomics also indicates skepticism toward a naive belief in progress. Maurice Godelier states that social evolution is not possible without retrogression and that it is impossible to speak of a "general evolution of humankind" (Godelier 1973, 128).

Analyzing the musical practice of a culture other than our own familiar one also requires that we relinquish the notion of linear "progress" for the present – at least until such a thesis becomes plausible in one or the other case, the possibility of which cannot, of course, be excluded. In principle, each musical practice must be understood within the overall cultural framework to which it belongs. The further we go back in history and the greater the gap between a culture under investigation and the main currents of international communication, the more distinctive the musical practice will be.

The cultures of various regions are often disparate, largely independent structures – a fact that makes the concept of a "universal history of music" so problematic. Universal concepts usually have their origins in the political, economic, and cultural interdependence of all countries. Yet because this global interdependence is a recent phenomenon, it cannot form the basis for analyzing cultural processes that took place prior to the establishment of a worldwide nexus. We must not under any circumstances derive principles of a "general" evolution from this perspective. The three-stages theory of Auguste Comte violated this guiding principle by presuming that all societies pass through certain phases, thereby furthering the view that this could also apply to music.

The Utility of a Global View

Once the naive evolutionary pattern has been rejected, we are entirely justified in proceeding to a global consideration. As far as I can see, this can be profitable in at least three instances:

1. Conceivably, historical developments of musical activity exist that lead from a common point of departure to different results or, vice

66

versa, that begin at different points and converge. For example, Hornbostel (1911) speaks of an acoustic criterion for cultural relations. A comparative method, which includes analysis of cultural forms of behavior in addition to acoustic-musical findings, is particularly rewarding in such cases. It is able to explain from the sociological point of view the extent to which historical musical convergence is contingent on social factors and the extent to which it can be seen as "coincidental," requiring further explanation.

2. All musical practices have to confront the problem of how to divide the octave, a division for which there is no physical-mathematical norm. Max Weber recommends examining how each musical practice deals with the fundamental contradictions inherent in the acoustic material. Joseph Yasser (1932) attempted – apparently without knowledge of Weber's ideas – to utilize this idea in order to understand the evolution of tonal systems. He was able to describe certain basic types of tonal system organization by means of logical analysis. In Weberian terms these models can be described as "ideal types," that is, as entities virtually nonexistent in reality in their pure form but which, applied cautiously, can be a helpful tool in investigating and illustrating. Useful as Yasser's models are, and much as they are able to stand up to empirical verification over a long period, they take little account of the "accidental forms" of the many tonal systems that are valid only within narrowly defined limits. Yasser could justify his hypothesis that tonal systems evolved in a universal pattern because, according to him, most of the "accidental" systems found in earlier forms of society were demonstrably incapable of winning acceptance beyond a small area. But the pentatonic solution of the fundamental acoustic contradiction was developed in more than one region of our planet, thereby proving the importance of this "ideal type" for actual development (Yasser 1932, 5 n.). From this point of view, it is appropriate to seek to create a theoretical pattern for a universal history of tonal systems. Such a pattern should neither guide nor replace field research in ethnomusicology. It should serve solely as an instrument of research, as a measuring instrument for empirically existing tonal systems.

3. Global aspects are likely to come to the fore where historical international interdependence exists, that is, during the era of

mediamorphosis at the latest. We are witnessing a worldwide hybridization of musical practices. It is obvious that this hybridization is being directed to a large degree by Western musical practice. The outcry is all too clear that the autochthonous musical cultures of the so-called Third World are being threatened or destroyed by the assault of the finished goods (sound recordings) distributed by the electronic media. The danger has been pointed out for Indian music, for example, that conformity to what is felt to be the "international Standard" will lead to the decay or loss of a wonderful and singular music (Daniélou 1975, 12). The Arab countries are also lamenting the decay of authentic music and the loss of tradition, to the point that most Arabs no longer know "genuine" Arab music (Touma 1975, 32).

There can be little doubt that non-Western cultures do not primarily desire the transition to Western musical practices for their own needs but that strong influences from outside create the loss of authentic traditions, the acceptance of Western models, or the development of hybrid practices. To be sure, endogenetic changes in the economic and social structure of these countries also play a role by encouraging urbanization and media saturation. Yet to a large extent these changes can also be attributed to external factors, be it colonialism, unthinking acceptance of Western technologies, or even so-called development aid. Regardless of the circumstances under which new social and technological structures are accepted, they always appear to be accompanied by at least a partial loss of musical identity. One does not have to support those who would like to protect cultural identity by erecting barriers against all industrialization in order to see this process as a task for music sociology.

The fact that the acceptance of Western practices often leads to different results in different regions gives music sociology virtually unprecedented opportunities to make intercultural comparisons by studying the effects of Western forms of behavior on traditional societies. A striking example is the transformation of Japanese musical culture over the past 150 years. One strongly suspects that Japanese society could have produced a musical practice similar to the Western one in parallel with their industrialization and without influences from the outside. To be sure, the Western model with its particular tonal system and instruments was presented in the Japanese educational system as early as 1879, and this may have accelerated the development. But the tempo with which "westernization" took place in Japan is evidence that forces in search of something new were already present within Japanese society.

As far as I know, Occidental observers did not predict this process. Had they been asked at the time how Japan's evolution into a mighty industrial giant might have affected international music, pundits would probably have predicted that Japanese music would conquer the world. That Japan has attained, by Occidental standards, a powerful status in musical education, concert life, instrument-making, and the electronic fixing, production, and diffusion of music without simultaneously establishing their own music the world over – this must have been as surprising to Western observers as the unexpected victory of the Japanese fleet over the Russians in 1905, which marked the actual beginning of history for modern Japan.

Tasks of Universal History

The study of the transformation of music during the transition from preindustrial to modern conditions is not only an important topic of a "world history of contemporary music"; it could also provide new knowledge in understanding the musical mutations of Occidental music itself, in grasping the musical mutations at the end of the European Middle Ages and at the beginning of the seventeenth century, for example. Of course, whatever benefit a global consideration of music can yield is merely a by-product. Those interested in a universal history of music have other interests. They are dedicated to comprehending the variety of given musical cultures and understanding the processes caused by global interdependence.

An example of such efforts is the Music in the Life of Man project undertaken by the International Music Council a good many years ago. It was pointed out at an early stage of this project that a universal history of music must not be content only to expound the forms and structures of different musics, but must also determine the roles that musical activity plays in various cultures at various times (Nketia 1980, 20). The sociological dimension of the project is thus indicated as well as its necessary methodological orientation: if musical activity can assume different functions, this means that the music-sociology method cannot be standardized but must be adapted to each musical culture under investigation. This point has been emphasized in a statement about the Music in the Life of Man project (Azevedo 1980, 59) and deserves to be underscored in light of the still widespread opinion that "music is the international language." The idea is itself a product of Occidental music history, because it is founded on Western-type performance music removed from a direct, confined social context. This does not, however, apply to what Pierre Joseph Proudhon called situational art (*art en situation*) in his 1865 book on the social vocation of art and what we would describe today with Besseler's term *participatory music*. "The concert is the death of music" (Proudhon 1971, 333) is a pointed way of expressing these circumstances; it alludes to the relaxation of the direct social referent and the relative autonomy of Occidental performance music, which is the exception, not the rule, in the universal history of music.

Research methods employed with a certain degree of success in studying relatively autonomous Western art music will not be adequate for participatory musics in life. It is remarkable that European musicology has also recently advocated broadening the field of study to music in life (cf. Flothius 1974), thereby aspiring to a closer connection between traditional historical research and the study of folk music and modern popular music.

Planning for the Music in the Life of Man project enlivened the discussion of methodological questions pertaining to a universal history of music. In 1989 a new basis was created for this project, administered by a Centre at the City University of New York, together with a new name – The Universe of Music: a History (UMH). An international team of scholars has been charged with publishing a twelve-volume universal history of music. The results of debates during the years of planning are reflected in the project description, emphasizing that the history is to be written by "authors native to the regions about which they write" and that the goal is "to capture the authentic voice of a people, to highlight the multiplicity as well as the diversity of musical phenomena, and to transmit a contextual understanding of music in life" (UMH, no.1, July 1990, 4).

The insistence on a "contextual understanding" seems to indicate the desired ethnological and sociological perspectives. The results will reveal the extent to which the aspects of mediamorphosis I have alluded to are treated. The idea of the global transformation made possible by technology strongly suggests itself, and is, as must be remarked with all due modesty, not new. As early as 1961, Walter Wiora recommended studying music from the point of view of the technological and industrial mutation. He spoke of the four ages of music, calling the fourth the age of technology and global industrial culture. The revolution brought about by this age leads not only to another change in Occidental music, comparable to the European changes around 1600 or 1750, but to a new international situation, to a "Europeanization" of the globe (Wiora 1961, 125-127).

Ethnomusicologists have accepted this process as an object of study, investigating the reactions to the Occidental influence. Bruno Nettl (1978b, 127) identifies three ideal-type reactions:

1. Preservation – aspiring to have the traditional culture remain intact
2. Complete westernization – simply incorporating the society into a Western cultural system
3. Modernization – adopting and adapting Western technology and other products of Western culture, as needed, while simultaneously insisting that the core of cultural values does not change greatly and in the end does not match those of the West

Nettl takes these tendencies as ideal-type constructs, made concrete in innumerable mixed forms. In individual cases it will no doubt be difficult to distinguish between westernization and modernization. As industrial civilization expands, the endogenous tendencies of modernization are also steered by "Occidental" forces from the outside. In the developing countries the logic of the industrial revolution usually does not take the form of a change from within but seems to be a transformation forced from the outside, as a break with the endogenous historical process (cf. Unesco 1980, 50, 274).

It would be tempting to attribute this break with tradition entirely to the technological-industrial factor. The fact must not be overlooked, however, that ideological goals also play a role. One of these notions is the tacit and unverified idea that the acquisition of Western modes of musical behavior is a form of "progress." That such a use of the term progress is more than questionable will have to be demonstrated by examples from tonal systems and notation.

Acculturation and its Repercussions

Regardless of how one evaluates this and similar mutations, one thing appears to be certain: a process of acculturation is taking place in many cultures under the clearly dominant influence of Occidental music. The most value-free description possible of the phenomenon is required in order to survey such acculturations scientifically. As Tran Van Khe has shown (1973, 199-200), it will not be easy to attribute to Western influence every disappearance of traditional-type music-making that results from industrialization. We must distinguish between describing the *phenomenon* of acculturation (namely, the adoption of foreign instruments, the modification of singing and playing styles, and the alteration of musical language or even tonal systems), investigating its *causes,* and determining its cultural *consequences*. There are two ideal-type classes of such cultural repercussions: (a) acculturation leading to impoverishment and possible loss of cultural identity and (b) acculturation understood and felt to be an enrichment.

This distinction taken from Tran Van Khe (1973, 207), however, cannot always be made. Furthermore, those affected would not always agree with the verdict of ethnomusicologists who attempt to identify loss or enrichment.

Does Occidental music contain aspects that virtually predestine it expand to other cultures? As far as I can tell, this question is seldom asked. Indian music has never been confined by the rhythmic corset of Western music, but Occidental music may have adopted its simpler metric patterns "in order to counterbalance the complicated harmonic and melodic structure of Western music" (Nijenhuis 1974, 60). By this schematization, Western music is suited to attracting other cultures, especially when just the simplified skeleton and not the harmonic richness that goes along with it is adopted. Wiora (1961, 131) believes, for example, that the eight-bar phrase in major, with its regular alternation of tonic and dominant, has comparable structures in all cultures, explaining why it was easily adopted.

Another aspect possibly conducive to the reception of Western music is the easily grasped rationality of the Western tonal system (and the notation associated with it). I have mentioned in connection with Adorno the phenomenon of the "resilience" of the Occidental tonal system and its inherent "tonality." This system has not only retained its dominant position again and again, in spite of innumerable innovations by Western avant-garde composers, it has also been able to extend its area of influence beyond Western culture. One might therefore ask whether it possesses expansive power as well as resilience. The fact that the number of people familiar with this type of "tonality" has grown by hundreds of millions since the beginning of the twentieth century might be used to support the hypothesis that the tonality has an inner attraction. One might, of course, object that the increasing dominance of Occidental tonality is the result, not of its "inner strength," but of the "external power" of processes of industrial technology that go hand in hand with the worldwide mediamorphosis. Neither the theoretical considerations of socio-musicologists nor the laboratory tests of musical psychologists can settle this. Not until we make a synthesis of many acculturation processes now taking place will we be able to come closer to answering this question.

The Role of Notation

An important criterion needed to define the special characteristics of a form of musical behavior is its relationship to notation. I have previously mentioned (chapter 19)[2] that the score as the end result of musical creation is a relatively recent phenomenon in Occidental music. Adorno had a simplifying, directly social explanation for the absence of score arrangement in Medieval European music. In his opinion, the handing down of music in parts and not in score could presumably be explained by the desire "to keep the *misera plebs* away from the alchemist's kitchen of counterpoint" (Adorno 1968, 115). Although secrecy played a role in a number of cultures, Adorno's interpretation is not adequate. As late as the sixteenth century, Europeans considered the score merely as a technical aid for the composer, not for music-making. The creation of the score had to be followed by its resolution into separate parts. The score itself was destroyed or erased, and the creator of the music communicated to the performers solely through the parts (cf. Georgiades 1958, 217).

2　Editorial note: Kurt Blaukopf is referring to the chapter "Mutations of Musical Behavior" in his book *Musical Life in a Changing Society: Aspects of Music Sociology* (Portland: 1992), 156–170.

Not until we understand the Western score as a late development will we be able to assess other musical cultures more accurately. Most of them regard as foreign not only the score but notation as well. As Daniélou remarks (1973, 63), the percentage of music in the world that can be written down is very small. Even placing bar lines can distort and destroy the melody when one attempts to notate such musics (cf. Graf 1965, 160). The symbols developed outside the musical culture with which we are familiar – roughly fifty such systems are known – serve primarily as aids to memory and not as a rational, unequivocal representation of music.

Of course, there is also evidence for Adorno's conjecture that symbols can occasionally be used to keep secrets. These proofs, however (taking no account of the not entirely explained meaning of *musica reservata*) refer to non-Western cultures. An approximately three-thousand-year-old Babylonian clay tablet containing texts and musical symbols closes with the note: "Secret. For initiate to show to initiate." It can be concluded from such sources (cf. Sachs 1968, 76-77) that the secret was not contained in the notation itself but in the ritual associated with the symbolized music.

The post-1600 Occidental notion according to which "musical creation" (= composition) takes place on music paper amounts to a reversal of the original relationship. The concept of "composition" could, with some justification, also be applied to music conceived without writing. Thus a book on Indian music speaks of "improvised composition," while vocal or instrumental improvisation lasting a number of hours is called "composition" (Nijenhuis 1974, 96).

Although the notation developed in India is an aid to memory, it has never evolved into a complete picture of music (Menon 1974, 64). The prerequisite for thinking in terms of notation, as established in the Occident, is the rationalization and standardization of the tonal system. This was the basis of Max Weber's idea that the rationalization of the tonal system and the attendant rationalization of notation was a specific feature of Occidental music. Recent sociology has picked up this idea again – without referring to Max Weber, yet based on the findings of ethnomusicology. Occidental notation is seen as a two-edged sword: as "progress" and "straitjacket": "Analytic notation has become a kind of grand-historical filter, selecting some elements of sound, those which it notates, to be of musical significance and others, those which it can notate only inadequately or not at all, as of only secondary importance for our perception of sound *as music*" (Wishart 1977, 135). We must, then, account for the fact that the possibilities of musical expression in our tonal system and notation are poorer in a number of respects than are those of musical cultures not bound by the constraints of our system. In this regard, then, the process of acculturation under Western influence must be termed "impoverishment" rather than "progress." The loss of expressive potential must thus be placed in the balance sheet alongside the enrichment by Occidental music. It is difficult to decide whether the sacrifice of microintervals and ornamental subtleties is compensated by the potential reception of chromatic harmony.

Even modern European musical history does not regard every achievement as purely positive. The progression from equal temperament, a prerequisite to chromatic harmony, has also resulted in a loss of expressive possibilities: "It is ironic that in equal temperament the increased freedom to modulate from one key to another is purchased at the expense of a lost distinction between these keys" (Benade 1976, 312).

When a musical culture built on oral tradition is confronted with the written music of the West, a rationalization of musical activity occurs that leads to the loss of particular musical messages for which the Western tonal and notational system has no place. Musical communication within Occidental cultures is not only made possible by the standardized division of the octave but by the absolute determination of pitches by international pitch (*Kammerton*), in force since the middle of the nineteenth century. Pitch fixation of this kind is, for example, unknown in Indonesian gamelan music: "No two gamelan slendro or gamelan pelog are tuned precisely the same" (Hood 1972, 5). This reveals its distance from Western thought just as clearly as, for example, the diversity of intervals in traditional Arab music which is far greater than that employed in the Western tonal system. The process of rationalization, reflected and solidified by our notation, harmonizes with the Occidental tendency to "demystify the world," as described a number of times by Max Weber (Weber 1973, 594). Ethnomusicology also interprets the transition from unwritten to written music as demystification in Weber's sense (cf. Blum 1978, 25-26).

Mediamorphosis intensifies this demystification on an international scale due to the weight of its musical "finished products," which obey the rationalized pattern of tonality and are offered as sound recordings and spread by means of ground and satellite broadcast. Technological development thus becomes a powerful force behind the increased worldwide dominance of the equal tempered twelve-pitch tonal system. It should not be overlooked, however, that new technical processes also contain a creative potential of possible benefit to both traditional and Western musical cultures.

Technological Processes as Creative Means

The synthetic production of sound could bring new elements into the present-day process of acculturation, for it also opens the possibility of preserving non-Western tonal systems and lends new impetus to their use. This is, for example, the basis of the hope that the "Indian way of hearing" may be retained through the technological production of Indian rhythmic models and Indian intervals (Ghatnekar 1975, 111). Having the ability to produce and store every kind of interval makes it tempting to construct equipment that can do justice to more than one tonal system. An example of such equipment is a device built for research into Indian music that is capable of reproducing fifty-two intervals within the octave (Cellier/Kudelski 1978). It can be used to produce intervals from the most varied musical cultures. To study Javanese music, a similar method that can simulate the "sound families" of many musical cultures was developed. The process defines "a set of synthetically generable sound events which are associated with an existing sound concept" (Jannssen/Kaegi 1986, 185).

This development reveals a surprising paradox: in the very epoch in which the pure special traits of non-Western musics are endangered, the new technological tool can help to preserve traditional tonal structures. Technological processes of this kind could also aid Western composers in defining where they stand. A number of attempts by twentieth-century composers to increase or refine the tonal resources of music have been blocked by the rigidity of the tonal system so deeply impressed on our consciousness. This system of norms, regardless of its undeniable aesthetic merits, excludes every subtler form of differentiation that may have been possible prior to the existence of these norms. Electronic sound production opens the door to new scales and new "sound families." Yet the works of electronic music that have been created since about 1950 seem to suggest that avant-garde composers have a hard time finding their way in an uncharted, endlessly large universe of sound and facilitating the access of listeners to this territory. Technological progress is supposed to enable composers to penetrate this broad area, yet they seem to lack a "cultural compass" which would enable them to take their bearings in this acoustical no-man's-land. The analysis of non-Western tonal systems in conjunction with efforts to understand forms of non-Western musical behavior could help the contemporary composer throw off the bonds of the accustomed tonal system to discover new musical resources. The builders of the equipment permitting fifty-two intervals within an octave have indicated the potential gain: "Based on observations on the psycho-physiological effect of intervals corresponding to precise numerical factors, this instrument presents new possibilities for the study of extra-European music. But it also offers a sound material extremely diversified and precise to the modern composer since it permits sound effects and expressive structures completely new" (Cellier/Kudelski 1978, 1).

The way opened by mediamorphosis, then, does not have to be a one-way street; it also offers possibilities for mutual illumination that can be of benefit to the West as well. Despite the present dominance of Western paradigms, this give-and-take could be profitable to both sides. The new technologies could, on the one hand, contribute to preserving the individuality of non-Western cultures and, on the other, make it easier for Western-trained composers to develop new musical resources.

There is no way to predict whether such a mutation of the musical material, of the tonal system and its use by the composer within Occidental culture, will occur. To be sure, a number of attempts of this kind have been made in recent decades, and some of these compositional projects are indubitably of artistic merit. Yet sociology cannot be satisfied with considering avant-garde composers alone; it must study the process in its totality. It thus becomes apparent that efforts by Occidental composers to refine their sonic raw material are not motivated entirely by the existence of new technological means. They go back further.

Anton Bruckner's enthusiasm for the just-tempered fifty-five-note harmonium of the Japanese Shohe Tanaka could be interpreted as the desire for a more subtle tonal system; Claude Debussy's wish for a division of the octave into twenty-one pitches points in the same direction; and Alban Berg's addition of plus and minus signs to a number of notes in order to indicate the desired departure from tempered intonation could also be taken as an attempt to break out of our tonal system.

Questions of this type have occasionally been studied following Joseph Yasser (1932, cf. Blaukopf 1972, 119-120). Arnold Schoenberg took a position on this problem (see Yasser 1953), yet to the best of my knowledge the literature has not dealt systematically with it or with the ideas of Bruckner, Debussy, and Alban Berg.

Western Copyright and Non-Western Reality

The traditional Western type of composer creates a written plan for the performance of his music. The written instructions he records on music paper enjoy the status of "works of art" comparable to the works of painters, sculptors, and writers. The Occident attributes to works of art aesthetic autonomy removed from reality, a view that forms part of a concept generally held by Occidental culture – that of a division between work and leisure, which results in a distinction between aesthetic experience and everyday experience. During the last two centuries the idea evolved that, although art could not regain freedom in practice, it could retain a kind of spiritual autonomy. According to this idea, receiving the message of art promotes the fraternity of mankind, as in the poem by Schiller that Beethoven set to music in his Ninth Symphony.

This accent on the liberating effect of the arts became one of the leitmotifs of European thought – in German Idealistic philosophy, in the literary works of John Ruskin and William Morris, or in the enthusiasm of Benedetto Croce for the non-logical nature of art. Croce wrote that "all the arts are music, if thereby we wish to give emphasis to the emotional origin of artistic images, excluding from their number those constructed mechanically or burdened with realism" (Croce 1983, 26). This value system, characteristic of European culture, secured for the work of art and its creator a high ideal value. Such attitudes also had practical consequences for the stance of society toward its artists, forming one of the bases for legal rules meant to provide moral and economic protection for the highly valued creations of artists. The so-called Bern Convention of 1886 (subsequently revised by later international agreements) was guided expressly by the desire "to protect in as effective and uniform a manner as possible the rights of authors over their literary and artistic works."

The copyright laws of individual states, as well as the international conventions governing copyright, are based on the Occidental idea of "intellectual property." According to this, the authors of musical works enjoy legal protection. They alone are given the right to control the public performance, reproduction, or arranging of their work. Indeed they even enjoy moral protection, for they have the right "to object to any distortion, mutilation, or other alteration" of their creations. In legal thought the work fixed in music notation was given the status of intellectual property. This Western concept is derived from the view that the composer's creative labor is expressed in the fully notated *res facto*. It is appropriate to use the Latin expression from the fifteenth century because it indicates the complete notation of the work as distinct from a merely fragmentary one that leaves room for improvisation.

The application of copyright principles oriented to such a *res facto* is characteristic of Western musical thought. Yet precisely this mode of thought creates problems when applied to non-Western musical cultures. The Western concept leads to a higher legal status being granted to the written form of aesthetically unpretentious music than to extremely artistic music developed without notation. By Western standards, a musician who has been creating non-notated music for many years and is able to perform it with extreme dexterity is not an author and is therefore unprotected. If, however, a far less artistically gifted musician manages to put that music, which he has not created, on paper he is considered the legal author entitled to the rights of use and economic benefits of the "work" he has "created."

The idea of the copyright protection of musical works evolved from the particular conditions of artistic creation in the Occident. The unmodified application of the concept to the musical life of other cultures contradicts their special needs and original values. Thus traditional, non-notated music can be mutilated and used for financial gain without out the creator of this music or the community to which this creator belongs receiving compensation. The electronic media offer ample opportunity for economically exploiting the non-notated musical legacy of other cultures.

Attempts have recently been made to put an end to this abuse. It appeared that not only is the problem acute in developing countries but the folk music of industrialized countries is subject to the same dangers from mediamorphosis. To counteract these dangers, a Fund for Folk Music was created in Sweden to which those who use collective (folk) musical property pay voluntary fees. Members of this free agreement include the Swedish Copyright Association, the phonograph industry, and the radio corporations.

The challenge to traditional music by mediamorphosis is also reflected in the legal measures of a number of developing countries. These measures are founded on the notion that the economic exploitation of collective musical property should entail fees, which in turn can be used to promote and develop the national musical culture. In Bolivia, for example, a 1968 state decree proclaimed traditional music to be part of the national legacy. This decree states that such music can be used in technological media only with the permission of the ethno-musicological department of the ministry of culture upon payment of a copyright fee. Monies thus earned are used to preserve the national musical legacy (cf. Aretz 1974, 123).

A similar attempt to extend copyright law to traditional music was made in Senegal in 1973. Among other things, this law states that commercial public performances or recordings of folk music require permission from the national collecting society, granted for a fee. The monies thus generated must be used for the benefit of authors.

A recent example of this new trend to confront the economic constraints of mediamorphosis is the copyright law that went into effect in Ghana in 1985. The law contains a noteworthy juristic innovation, stating that the rights to folklore belong to the state "as if the Republic were the original creator of the work." To my knowledge, this statement is the clearest to date of the notion that the state, as representative of the collectivity, is entitled to act on behalf of the (usually anonymous) creators of folk music.

Laws of this kind clearly reveal the difference between Western notions of law on the one hand and the needs of developing countries on the other. It seems difficult for Western minds to grasp this difference. In order to do so a correct description and evaluation of traditional musical activity is required. Can it be called creative or is it merely repetitive? Are we permitted to judge the creative importance of this kind of musical activity by its originality and innovation, as in the West, or do other criteria apply? These questions are of importance not only for the music, but for the entire area of arts and crafts in non-Western countries, and they have been asked a number of times about African cultures. The answers are also valid for music in traditional cultures. In these cultures creativity is not synonymous with innovation and originality: "The creativity comes rather through the individual development of particular skills in organizing or performing something that is essentially traditional" (Ottenberg 1975, 215-216).

Our aesthetic and legal notions derived from notated music are unable to do justice to the diversity of cultures. The call for new legal regulations is long overdue because the dynamic of mediamorphosis has turned the attack by Western norms on the musical cultures of other societies into a central problem, one that can be solved (cf. Blaukopf 1990).

The Occidental understanding of the musical work as a *res facto*, a work complete for all times, clashes with the understanding many other cultures have of music. It also entails a different understanding of musical time. The precise definition of "beginning" and "end" of music is not universal.

Music and Time

Very frequently participatory music in life does not derive its beginning and end from musical structure but rather from the logic of the event of which it is a part. The obligatory rules characteristic of Western culture do not apply even to liturgy linked to a text. The recitation of the Koran can begin in the middle of a Sura and stop before its end (Touma 1975, 142). The question of how the musics of foreign cultures are heard and how unexpected musical experiences fit into one's own overall experiences has, to the best of my knowledge, yet to be investigated systematically. An instructive illustration is found in the reactions of a European who, when confronted for the first time with Indian music, recognizes no clear divisions between "warming up" (e.g., tuning the instruments) and the "performance." He patiently waits for the beginning only to find out suddenly "that the performance *has* in fact already begun" (Crossley-Holland 1966, 105).

Participatory music must also not take its orientation from the familiar notion of length of performance. Every attempt to separate such music from its situational context and to describe it "in itself," without taking into account the non-musical elements of what is going on, is a violation of its nature. Even the otherwise praiseworthy efforts of ethnologists to rescue traditional music from oblivion via tape recordings runs into this cultural barrier. It has been shown, for example, that adapting performances of traditional Korean music to the playing time of a record falsifies it (Hey Ku Lee 1975, 57-58). The process of mediamorphosis, then, affects everything down to ethnological studies, because the technological fixation of music not only preserves the traditional material but distorts it as well. This distortion effect has also been verified for Iranian classical music (Nettl 1978a, 156).

The technological recording of traditional music, then, tendentially alters its function. Music that is meant to be embedded in a given pattern of activity becomes independent of such patterns and has imposed upon it a beginning and an end, which are nonexistent in traditional music-making and listening. At the same time, mediamorphosis brings about a new proximity of music to life. Portable radios and cassette players, equipment which has penetrated into the everyday life of Arab nomads, turn the broadcast schedule of radio stations into the regulator of the daily routine (Chabrier 1974, 39). Program announcements and jingles mark periods of time, yet the music acts as a disjointed background. This music can be either Western-style notated "works" or traditional in origin. It attains, however, a new directness, entering the life of the listeners and altering their daily rhythm. The impact on non-Western cultures of messages transported by the electronic media can be called "secondary orality," to use a fitting expression of Walter J. Ong: Electronic technology "has brought us into the age of 'secondary orality'. This new orality has striking resemblances to the old in its participatory mystique, its fostering of a communal sense, its concentration on the present moment, and even its use of formulas. But it is essentially a more deliberate and self-conscious orality, based permanently on the use of writing and print, which are essential in the manufacture and operation of the equipment and for its use as well" (Ong 1988, 136). Ong has devoted his attention to the technologizing of the word. It also seems useful to apply these thoughts to the technologizing of music, because they indicate a characteristic feature of mediamorphosis, a secondary ordering of life governed by the electronic media. This "secondary orality" of musical communication is particularly noticeable in non-Western cultures, yet the fact should not be overlooked that it has long since taken hold of musical practice in the industrialized countries, where almost all popular music, and even part of the electronically mediated folk music and art music, is under its influence (cf. Blaukopf 1980, 19-20).

Tonal Character of the Singing Voice

The intrusion of Western practices into other musics presumably fosters an assimilation in the use of the singing voice. The existing differences are a warning against viewing all musics from a standard point of view. If a European listener considers the voice of an Indian singer forced and nasal, he seldom takes into consideration that to Indian listeners the European style of singing can seem "unnatural." The Western style of singing appears not to have fully prevailed until rather late (perhaps not until the seventeenth century). The findings of ethnomusicology indicate that large regions (e.g., the Near East) prefer nasal, throaty singing. The question of how universally this type of singing was practiced in the European Middle Ages has been studied a number of times (cf. Marquardt 1936, Müller-Heuser 1963). The representation of the distorted faces of angels by the brothers Van Eyck on the Ghent Altar (ca. 1430) has been interpreted as implying a nasal tonal ideal (Sachs 1959, 16-17).

What could be the social motivation of such a vocal tone? What social meaning could there be behind this norm? A hypothetical explanation has been offered for Arab-Islamic music that may be applicable to other cultures: the singer's "supernatural" inspiration prohibits him from using every-day intonation, requiring instead a supernatural, that is, an unnatural voice (Hickmann 1970, 56-57). This hypothesis once again points to the social function of musical activity as a factor that can influence activity down to the smallest details. The extent to which the acculturation accelerated by mediamorphosis may decrease or even eliminate the variety of vocal styles in the world remains an open question, one which the universal history of music will certainly seek to answer. This question is linked to a problem that the contemporary literature calls a problem of "cultural identity." The possible loss of these cultural identities through the process of acculturation has only recently begun to concern sociologists, whereas ethnologists have been dealing with it for quite some time.

83

Cultural Identity

The slogan of preserving cultural identity has recently become fashionable. We have slowly begun to realize, however, that the notion of cultural identity must be defined more exactly and that not everything belonging to this identity is necessarily worth preserving. The satirical songs about criminals at their public execution, sung well into the nineteenth century, may have belonged to the "cultural identity" of some nations; nonetheless, civilized countries today are glad that both the national ritual of execution and a good many barbaric songs have been forgotten.

We must therefore be careful in using the concept of cultural identity. The idea that everything should be preserved was compatible with the long-since obsolete idea of the "ahistoricity" of traditional cultures, but this is no longer consistent with a dynamic view of cultural activity. The recurrent lamentation in the ethnological literature over the decline of traditional music-making must also be seen from this viewpoint. Thus, at a symposium in Dakar (Senegal), an African musician asked the entirely justifiable question how it was conceivable that Africa could develop politically and socially while at the same time clinging unchanged to its musical tradition (Bebey 1979, 139). That which an African nation considers to be its musical advantage should not be determined by ethnologists, no matter how well-intentioned, but by those affected. They are entitled to decide how much modernization or westernization is desirable. Thus the idea that the seven-tone scale is more "progressive" than the pentatonic scale (Bebey 1979, 135) may be considered an abandonment of musical identity by some ethnologists, yet those who understand the mechanisms of social change will not be as surprised.

Even political thought seems to consider awareness of national identity entirely compatible with the spectacular acceptance of foreign forms of behavior. I therefore do not share the astonishment of an ethnologist who writes about music in the Philippines: "It is curious to note that some youthful nationalists listen more to rock music than to Philippine folk or Western classical music" (Maceda 1972, 39). The adaptation to Western patterns of the national anthems of numerous countries also betrays the combining of national ambitions with musical acculturation (cf. Blaukopf 1978).

A number of forms of originally Western behavior assume entirely new functions in the context of Third World national movements. The musicians of these nations are often even proud of not only being inundated by acculturation but of taking part in it, perhaps creatively. They do not regard it as a loss of cultural identity. They do not want outside observers to define the authentic aspects of their culture; authentic is defined as "what they really are" (Bebey 1979, 139). Statements of this kind show that many musicians in developing nations regard acculturation not as an entirely negative phenomenon but also as a challenge. This confirms the correctness of the distinction made in ethnomusicology between *passive* and *active* acculturation (cf. Gerson-Kiwi 1973, 187).

Active acculturation covers the demand heard in a number of developing countries for balanced communication with all musical cultures. The encounter with Western music is not rejected; one merely attempts to reduce it to a degree compatible with the principle of balanced international exchange. This tendency was clearly present in Nigeria during the seventies. After achieving independence (1960), this African country with a population of about seventy million underwent rapid economic, political, and cultural development, owing primarily to its reserves of raw materials. The musical consequences of this development were reflected in the *Nigerian Music Review*, founded in 1977. Not surprisingly, this country whose official language is English, alongside a multitude of local languages, also advocated the idea of "polyglot" music because the presence of foreign elements in the culture was not necessarily regarded as negative. Fears of a musical "colonization" of Nigeria were therefore rejected as unfounded, with one exception: foreign pop music (Euba 1977, 19).

Leveling and its Limits

In the cultural policy of a number of countries, the dominant influence of Western popular music has led to measures directed at weakening its leveling effects. For example, there were occasional demands for import restrictions on recordings of Western popular music, or calls for restrictions on radio programs. In 1980 Kenya attempted to begin a "national renaissance" of music by a government decree proclaiming that seventy-five percent of the music played on the radio had to be performed by Kenyan musicians. The experiment was a failure, and the decree had to be annulled. It was shown that restrictive measures by themselves were not sufficient and had to be accompanied by positive promotion of native music to be successful.

The transfer of the technologies of electronic production and reproduction of music also allows developing countries the opportunity to play an active role in the acculturation process. Even where this possibility has not been taken advantage of, total westernization and leveling (to the best of present knowledge) does not have to take place. A study of the role played by the music industry in the present-day transformation leads to the prediction of two possible outcomes: "A global music culture available to almost everybody [will be attained] long before a corresponding worldwide homogeneity in languages, living conditions, etc. is reached. . . . [Or] a multitude of types of music arising out of new living conditions and new music technologies [will emerge], at the same time as traditional music is adapted to new environments where, albeit with some changes, it can be put to similar uses and functions as in traditional society" (Wallis/Malm 1984, 324).

Investigation of the Western elements that penetrate non-Western music comes to a similar conclusion. According to Nettl (1985) these elements include functional harmony developed in Occidental music, notation and the idea of the integrity of the "work of music," and the adoption of Western instruments. Because musical practice still provides room for the expression of individual identity, it is still possible for cultural entities, social classes, certain age groups, and minorities to retain elements of their particular repertoires and musical styles. Were one to attempt to draw a conclusion from these processes about the reaction of world cultures to the invasion of Western music, one could say "that each [culture] has tried, sometimes at great cost, to retain some significant degree of musical identity; and that each has found ways to symbolize, in its music, the positive, negative, and ambiguous aspects of its relationship to European-derived lifeways and values" (Nettl 1985, 165).

Whatever course "international music" will take in the future, technological evolution will play a crucial role; this justifies describing the process as mediamorphosis. Of course, we must make sure not to overrate the role of technology as if it were the single, inevitable determinant of cultural events. There can be no doubt that the tool we have created in turn gains power over us. "But technology alone will not decide the outcome. People and governments do that" (Wallis/Malm 1984, 324).

Despite the vast force of mediamorphosis and its palpable effects on musical activity on a world scale, it is no guarantee that our planet must be transformed into the "global village" of Marshall McLuhan. Despite standardization of economic and technological processes, countless differences will persist in the living conditions of peoples. Abstract patterns of the changes caused by mediamorphosis are unable to do justice to these differences. The climatic conditions of social life are themselves so diverse from region to region that no general standardization of cultural forms of behavior can be expected. The French writer Albert Camus once said that one of the world's many injustices, the injustice of climate, is never discussed (Camus 1961, 37). If we replace the word "injustice" with "differences" we can see that not only economic, social, and political factors are interwoven in the structure of conditions of cultural life, but climatic ones as well. The "natural" environment is one of these factors – the composition of the landscape, the climatic zone to which it belongs, the weather conditions, and so on.

This idea was not introduced by sociologists. It was present in the writings of Hegel and Marx, just as it was contained in the idea of "milieu" as used by Hippolyte Taine. Japanese culturology has rightly made a central concept of "fudo." This word can only be approximately translated as "climate," because it fuses the features of a culture with the natural phenomena of weather and geography (East Asia 1975). On the whole, Occidental culture belongs to the temperate climatic zone. This also explains why Occidental thought is largely unfamiliar with a theoretical construct that combines natural and cultural aspects, one well suited to describing factors that control the course of musical mutations. The continuing variety of climates in this sense will also, in my opinion, tend to limit leveling on an international scale. This could ensure for quite some time to come the existence of the pluralism cherished by advocates of cultural identities.

This statement once again supports my wish for the variety of methodologies appropriate to the universal history of music. The concept of global mediamorphosis does not conflict with this demand. It is not to be taken as a "law," but merely as a hypothesis that may be falsified by empirical research.

Bibliography

Adorno, Theodor W., *Impromptus* (Frankfurt am Main: 1968).

Aretz, Isabel, "Music in Latin America: The Perpetuation of Tradition", *Cultures*, vol. 1, no. 3, 1974, 117–131.

Azevedo, Luis Heitor Correa de, "Preliminary study on the project of preparing a Universal History of Music and on the role of the music of Latin America and the Caribbean in this history", *The World of Music*, vol. 22, no. 3, 1980, 56–65.

Bebey, Francis, "African musical tradition in the face of foreign influence", *Cultures*, vol. 6, no. 2, 1979, 132–140.

Benade, Arthur H., *Fundamentals of Musical Acoustics* (New York: 1976).

Blaukopf, Kurt, "Hymnen", *HiFi-Sterophonie*, 8/1972, 708.

Blaukopf, Kurt, "Nationalhymnen der Dritten Welt: Kulturelle Identität oder Anpassung an 'westliche' Normen", *HiFi-Sterophonie* 17/1978, 540.

Blaukopf, Kurt, "Akustische Umwelt und Musik des Alltags", in Reinhold Brinkmann (ed.), *Musik im Alltag* (Mainz: 1980).

Blaukopf, Kurt, *Beethovens Erben in der Mediamorphose: Kultur- und Medienpolitik für die elektronische Ära* (Heiden: 1989).

Blaukopf, Kurt, "Legal Policies for the Safeguarding of Traditional Music: Are They Utopian?" *The World of Music*, vol. 32, no. 1, 1990, 125–133

Blum, Stephen, "Changing roles of performers in Meshhed and Bojnurd, Iran", in Bruno Nettl (ed.), *Eight Urban Musical Cultures* (Urbana: 1978).

Camus, Albert, *Kleine Prosa* (Reinbek: 1961).

Cellier, Claude / Kudelski, André, *The S 52: A New Electronic Instrument for Musical Research* (Lausanne: 1978).

Chabrier, Jean-Claude, "Music in the Fertile Crescent: Lebanon, Syria, Iraq", *Culture*, vol. 1, no. 3, 1974, 35–58.

Croce, Benedetto, *Guide to Aesthetics* (Lanham: 1983).

Crossley-Holland, Peter, "Problems and Opportunities in Listening to the Music of Another Civilisation", in Indian Council for Cultural Relations (ed.), *Music East and West* (New Delhi: 1966).

Daniélou, Alain, *Die Musik Asiens zwischen Mißachtung und Wertschätzung* (Wilhelmshaven: 1973).

Daniélou, Alain, *Einführung in die indische Musik* (Wilhelmshaven: 1975).

East Asian Cultural Studies, "The Present State of Research on Cultural Development in Japan", *East Asian Cultural Studies*, vol. 14 (Tokyo: 1975).

Euba, Akin, "An Introduction to Music in Nigeria", *Nigerian Music Review*, 1/1977.

Flothius, Marius, *Taken van de hedendaagse musicoloog*, inaugural address given at the University of Utrecht, 1974.

Frederickson, Jon, "Technology and Music Performance in the Age of Mechanical Reproduction", *International Review of the Aesthetics and Sociology of Music*, vol. 20, no. 2, 1989, 193–220.

Georgiades, Thrasybulos, "Zur Lasso-Gesamtausgabe", in *Bericht über den Internationalen Musikwissenschaftlichen Kongreß in Wien 1956* (Graz: 1958).

Gerson-Kiwi, Edith, "The Musician in Society: East and West", *Cultures*, vol. 1, 1973, 165–193.

Ghatnekar, V. V., "Automatic Production of Music", in B. C. Deva (ed.), *Musical Scales* (New Delhi: 1975).

Godelier, Maurice, *Ökonomische Anthropologie: Untersuchungen zum Begriff der sozialen Struktur primitiver Gesellschaften* (Reinbek: 1973).

Graf, Walter, "Die vergleichende Musikwissenschaft an der Universität Wien", *Mitteilungen der Anthropologischen Gesellschaft in Wien*, vol. 95, 1965, 155–161.

Hey Ku Lee, "Impact of Western Music an Asian Music", in *Proceedings of the First Asian Pacific Music Conference* (Seoul: 1975), 54–60.

Hickmann, Hans, "Die Musik des arabisch-islamischen Bereichs", in Hans Hickmann / Wilhelm Staude (eds.), *Orientalische Musik* (Leiden: 1970).

Hood, Mantle, "Music of Indonesia", in B. Spuler et. al (eds.), *Handbuch der Orientalistik*, sec. 3, vol. 6 (Leiden: 1972).

Hornbostel, Erich M., "Über ein akustisches Kriterium für Kulturzusammenhänge", *Zeitschrift für Ethnologie*, 43/1911, 601–615.

Jannssen, J. / Kaegi, H., "MIDIM-duplication of a Central Javanese Sound Concept", *Interface: Journal of New Music Research* 15/1986, 185–229.

Lévi-Strauss, Claude, "Race and History", in Leo Kuper (ed.), *Race, Science and Society* (London: 1975).

Lorenz, Konrad, *Das Wirkungsgefüge der Natur und das Schicksal des Menschen: Gesammelte Arbeiten* (Munich: 1978).

Maceda, José, "Music in the Philippines", in B. Spuler et. al (eds.), *Handbuch der Orientalistik* (Leiden: 1972).

Marquardt, P., *Der Gesang und seine Erscheinungsformen im Mittelalter*, PhD-thesis (Berlin: 1936).

Menon, Narayana,"Music and Culture Change in India", *Cultures*, vol. 1, no. 3, 1974, 59–64.

Müller-Heuser, Franz, *Vox humana: Ein Beitrag zur Untersuchung der Stimmästhetik des Mittelalters* (Regensburg: 1963).

Nettl, Bruno, *Persian Classical Music in Tehran: The Process of Change* (Urbana: 1978a).

Nettl, Bruno, "Some Aspects of the History of World Music in the Twentieth Century: Questions, Problems and Concepts", *Ethnomusicology*, 22/1978b, 123–136.

Nettl, Bruno, *The Western Impact on World Music* (New York: 1985).

Nijenhuis, Emmie te, "Indian Music: History and Structure", in B. Spuler et. al (eds.), *Handbuch der Orientalistik*, sec. 2, vol. 6 (Leiden: 1974).

Nketia, Joseph H. Kwabena, "Africa in the World of Music", *The World of Music*, vol.22, no. 3, 1980, 19–28.

Ong, Walter J., *Orality and Literacy: The Technologizing of the Word* (London: 1988).

Ottenberg, Simon, *Masked Rituals of Afikpo: The Context of African Art* (Seattle: 1975).

Proudhon, Pierre-Joseph, *Du principe de l'art et de sa destination sociale* [orig. 1865] (Farnborough: 1971).

Sachs, Curt, *Vergleichende Musikwissenschaft: Musik der Fremdkulturen* (Heidelberg: 1959).

Sachs, Curt, *Die Musik der Alten Welt* (Berlin: 1968).

Sorce Keller, Marcello, "Sociology of Music and Ethnomusicology: Two Disciplines in Competition", *The Journal of General Education*, vol. 38, no. 3, 1986, 167–181.

Touma, Habib Hassan, *Die Musik der Araber* (Wilhelmshaven: 1975).

Tran van Khe "Traditional Music and Culture Change: A Study in Acculturation", *Cultures*, vol. 1, no. 1, 1973, 195–210.

UMH, *The Universe of Music: A History.* (Newsletter publ. annually by the Center for Music Research and Documentation, City University of New York, July 1990)

UNESCO, *Preliminary Report of the Director General on the Medium-Term Plan for 1984–1989* (1982).

Wallis, Roger / Malm, Krister, *Big Sounds from Small Peoples: The Music Industry in Small Countries*, Series of reports from the Gothenburg University Department of Musicology, no. 7 (London: 1984).

Weber, Max, *Gesammelte Aufsätze der Wissenschaftslehre* (Tübingen: 1973).

Wiora, Walter, *Die vier Weltalter der Musik* (Stuttgart: 1961).

Wishart, Trevor, "Musical Writing, Musical Speaking", in John Shepherd et al. (eds.), *Whose Music: A Sociology of Musical Languages* (London: 1977).

Yasser, Joseph, *A Theory of Evolving Tonality* (New York: 1932).

Yasser, Joseph, "A Letter from Arnold Schoenberg", *Journal of the American Musicological Society*, vol. 6, no. 1, 1953, 53–62.

Part IV
Sociology and the Philosophy
of Science

The Sociological Concept of the *Kunstwollen* and its Origins in the Austrian School of Art History and Musicology[1]

Music sociology is sometimes accused of not having firmly established its repertoire of methods.[2] Such an accusation is based on the assumption that musicology can draw its sociological tools from sociology in useable finished parts. This expectation clouds the view for the sociological questions and methods that do not stem from theories in sociology but have been developed by musicology itself. This includes the theory of *Kunstwollen*[3] and its linking with empirical research, as it was developed by the Vienna art historian Alois Riegl (1858–1905) and taken into the methods of musicology by Guido Adler. This concept is inseparably linked with a style of thought that in Adler's surroundings the natural sciences, jurisprudence and above all the Vienna School of Art History were attached to.

Alois Riegl's pupil Hans Tietze wrote a *Method of Art History*,[4] which Guido Adler's *Method of Music History*[5] picked up, not only echoing the title but in its content. Both methods were based on the idea that the social (and thereby also artistic) processes are accessible to scientific analysis. Adler's friend and patron, the physicist Ernst Mach, had already argued this thesis in 1863, in his *Lectures on Psychophysics*, and in particular had pointed to the application of statistical methods and their use in the understanding of such processes. The strict separation of the so-called exact sciences from the cultural sciences had no place in this concept. Nothing that was typical of a particular genre of science was strict – Mach believed – because the words "exact" and "not exact" simply marked stages of development of every discipline.[6]

---

1   Editorial note: first published in *Musiktheorie*, yr. 5., no. 3, 1990, 195–203.
2   cf. Carl Dahlhaus / Günter Meyer, "Musiksoziologische Reflexionen", in Carl Dahlhaus / Helga de la Motte-Haber (eds.), *Systematische Musikwissenschaft*, series "Neues Handbuch der Musikwissenschaft" vol. 10 (Wiesbaden / Laaber: 1982), 109.
3   Editorial note: see also footnote 16, page 46f.
4   Hans Tietze, *Die Methode der Kunstgeschichte* (Leipzig: 1913).
5   Guido Adler, *Methode der Musikgeschichte* (Leipzig: 1919).
6   cf. Wolfram W. Swoboda, "Physik, Physiologie und Psychophysik", in

Since Ernst Mach had demanded that the "laws" of natural science should be understood as falsifiable "principles",[7] the possible convergence of natural science and cultural science, which Guido Adler also regarded as desirable, came to light in this style of thought: "Perhaps the two lines, natural science and historical research, which previously ran parallel to one another at a certain distance, will in the future tend towards one another and will meet each other."[8]

Guido Adler indicated how the relationship between theory formation (i.e. the setting up of "principles") and empirical research should be understood. For him it was clear that there were no unchangeable criteria of artistic beauty[9] and that it was the task of research to uncover the respective manifestations of the "art ideal". Adler used the term *Kunstwollen* for such manifestations of the "art ideal".[10]

The term *Kunstwollen* as a construction to be gained from empirical research as an ideal type became an instrument of music sociological research. Strangely, this has so far hardly been noted in the methodological discussion, although the relation of this way of thought to Max Weber's sociology is noticeable down to the area of its terminology. If one follows this trail, then the specific contribution of aesthetics and musicology to the sociology of art and music can be identified.

The theory of *Kunstwollen* goes back to Alois Riegl. In *Stilfragen* [*Problems of Style*], published in 1893, whose ideas were echoed in Guido Adler, Riegl was already proposing the view that the whole of art history represented a continuous struggle with the material: "it is not the tool – which is determined by the technique – but the artistically creative idea."[11] Riegl's attempt empirically to establish the transition from the ancient ideals of art to the later "ugliness and lifelessness" on the basis of the products of the "late Roman art industry" was based, as he later expressed it, on a teleological understanding of the creation

Rudolf Haller / Friedrich Stadler (eds.), *Ernst Mach – Werk und Wirkung* (Vienna: 1988), 363f.

7   Ernst Mach, *The History and the Root of the Principle of the Conservation of Energy* (Chicago: 1911), 4.
8   Guido Adler, "Methode der Musikgeschichte", op. cit., 35.
9   ibid., 121.
10   ibid., 9f., 143, 183.
11   Alois Riegl, *Problems of Style: Foundations for a History of Ornament* (Princeton: 1992), 33.

of art. He saw the work of art as "the result of a definite and purposeful *Kunstwollen* which makes its way forward in the struggle with function, raw material and technique".[12] Thus, in this "teleological" understanding, what from the standpoint of a modern observer may appear as ugliness and lifelessness does not represent the result of lack of ability but rather the result of the artistic intention.

Accordingly, art research is concerned with the exploration of the intention, the *Kunstwollen*. Such thinking has long been taken for granted in ethnomusicology as much as in music sociology, and in the thinking of the history of music the idea of the continuous historical advance towards a highest ideal – an idea to which Kretzschmar was still attached – has been replaced by other concepts. The coming together of the historical and the ethnographic approaches results from this: music history and ethnomusicology are concerned with "different" musical cultures, and this difference is based simply on the temporal or spatial distance, which does not justify separating "systematic" research from the "historical". The attempt at such a separation – Gilbert Chase believes – would even represent a step behind Guido Adler's concept.[13]

For Adler, in the conceptual development based on the first outline of his discipline,[14] the concept of *Kunstwollen* played a decisive role. Riegl's disciple Hans Tietze (1880–1954), to whom Adler expressly referred, provided the connection to the Austrian School of Art History for Adler. Tietze clarified the concept of *Kunstwollen* as a "synthesis of the artistic expressions of a time"[15] and clearly distinguished this empirically achieved synthesis from speculative constructions such as *Zeitgeist* or *Volksgeist*: "Here it is . . . not a case of a particular mystical force, about an urge of a people . . . but about a term that has been distilled solely from the works and other statements, which serves for the orientation of all new additional individual objects but which can also experience further extension and modification from them."[16]

---

12 Alois Riegl, *Late Roman Art Industry* (Rome: 1985), 9.
13 Gilberi Chase, "Musicology, History, and Anthropology", in John W. Grubbs (ed.), *Current Thought in Musicology* (Austin: 1975), 233.
14 Guido Adler, "Umfang, Methode und Ziel der Musikwissenschaft", *Vierteljahrsschrift für Musikwissenschaft*, 1 / 1885, 5–20.
15 Tietze, *Methode der Kunstgeschichte*, op. cit., 13f.
16 ibid., 14.

The serviceability of the term *Kunstwollen* as a tool of art history was frequently discussed by Alois Riegl. However, the fact that Riegl's concept not only found its way into Adler's method but also into the thinking of Max Weber, and thereby became an integral component of the Weberist sociology of art has previously attracted little attention.

Riegl's ideas found their way to Max Weber through Georg Lukács, who made a work available to Weber that he had started in 1912 and which was only published posthumously, under the title *The Heidelberg Philosophy of Art*.[17] In this text Lukács draws attention to the "important approaches to a philosophy of the history of art that emerged with Riegl".[18] In a letter to Lukács on 10 March 1913, Weber, whose curiosity about Riegl had obviously been awoken, wrote: "Riegl . . . I do not know, to my shame it should be said."[19]

The traces of Max Weber's subsequent occupation with the ideas of Alois Riegl are evident. They are most apparent in Weber's presentation of the problem of remaining value-free in the social sciences, which he gave as a lecture in Vienna in 1913 and published in revised form in 1917.[20]

In this text, Weber did not simply take up the term *Kunstwollen*, but also – entirely in Riegl's sense – traced the relationship of the *Kunstwollen* to the technical preconditions of its accomplishment. The concept of "progress" – according to Weber – was indeed not applicable to art itself, but certainly to the "establishment of the technical means which a certain type of artistic impulse applies when the end is definitely given". Here Weber came to the methodologically significant conclusion that: "'Technical' progress, correctly understood, does indeed belong to the domain of art history, because it (and its influence on the artistic impulse) is a type of phenomenon which is determinable in a strictly empirical way, i.e., without aesthetic evaluation."[21]

---

17 Georg Lukacs, *Heidelberger Philosophie der Kunst*, in: id., *Werke*, vol. 16, (Darmstadt: 1974).
18 ibid., 39.
19 Georg Lukács, *Briefwechsel 1902–1917* (Budapest: 1982), 320.
20 Editorial note: Max Weber, "The Meaning of 'Ethical Neutrality' in Sociology and Economics", in id., *Max Weber on the Methodology of the Social Sciences*, translated and edited by Edward A. Shils and Henry A. Finch (Glencoe: 1949), 1–47.
21 Max Weber, "The Meaning of 'Ethical Neutrality'", op. cit., (Glencoe: 1949), 29.

Weber was by no means satisfied with this general thesis, but also gave examples for the methodical separation of *Kunstwollen* on the one hand and technical conditions on the other.

a)   The meeting of the technical construction conditions of Gothic architecture with the "content of feelings" conditioned by the sociological and religious history of the Gothic epoch;

b)   the interaction of technological rationalisation of the tonal system in occidental music with the *Kunstwollen* aimed at the development of third in a harmonic sense, and

c)   the contribution of such an empirical approach to the understanding of the development of painting, which he regarded as being validated by Heinrich Wölfflin's work *Die klassische Kunst* (1899) [Classic Art].[22]

This kind of interdisciplinary approach is characteristic of Max Weber. Given the state of things, it could have been fruitful precisely in the circle of Austrian art history and musicology, but the dialogue that Guido Adler had opened up with Riegl's school hardly seems to have been continued. One exception was the Vienna art historian Otto Benesch (1896–1964), who analysed Weber's posthumously published work *The Rational and Social Foundations of Music*.[23] In the process he undertook the attempt to explain the general significance of Weber's music-sociology work "by exemplifying its findings in the . . . field of fine arts".[24]

The methodological basic position of numerous works in the field of music sociology is based on the conceptual separation of the technical-rational findings from the *Kunstwollen* that was undertaken by Riegl, Adler and Weber with the aim of apprehending the significance of technical conditions for changes in the *Kunstwollen*.

This way of thinking does not even ask the question of what is "more decisive" – the *Kunstwollen* or the technology – at all. The theory of the *Kunstwollen* renounces the establishment of a fixed causality. In this, too, it corresponds to natural-science thinking, as it was represented above all by Ernst Mach. Mach replaced the concept of causality by that

---

22   ibid., 29.

23   Max Weber, *The Rational and Social Foundations of Music*, translated and edited by D. Martindale, J. Riedel and G. Neuwirth (Carbondale: 1958).

24   Otto Benesch, "Max Weber als Musikwissenschaftler", *Österreichische Rundschau*, 1918 (1922), 389f.

of function.[25] This understanding can be found again in the *methods* of Guido Adler and Hans Tietze – with the express mention of Mach. Max Weber's sociology, too, contents itself with signalling the "encounter", the "interaction" or the "meeting" of a particular *Kunstwollen* with particular technological circumstances and portraying the functional connection in such a way (without from the beginning posing the question of causality, which of course could ultimately be answered by empirical research).

This methodological outline, which contrasts the *Kunstwollen* with the instruments available for its manifestations, certainly grants the *Kunstwollen* a certain priority (without *Kunstwollen* no artistic act), but it also again outlines the role of technology that is available to artistic creation in each case. According to this, the technological means determine the potential that can be utilised by the *Kunstwollen* and again also mark out the limits for the realisation of the *Kunstwollen*. Thus, for example, the *Musikwollen* in occidental history was striving for an interpretation of the third in the harmonic sense long before the available tonal system had changed from the diatonic to the harmonic determination of the third. The musical impulse had the technical possibilities at its disposal that could lead to unlimited harmonic modulation – up to the *Tristan* harmonic – when this harmonic understanding had asserted itself in the scale system and finally led to its rationalisation in the sense of an equal temperature. Similarly, the *Kunstwollen* aiming at linear perspective in pictorial representation was also recognisable before the rules of perspective had been developed. With the use of several vanishing points, the portrayal of space in the picture was moving towards linear perspective, until one day it was not the painters but the architects and engineers who developed the system of this perspective, and the painters were able to put it at the service of their art.

Occasionally the impulses for a changed *Kunstwollen* seem to stem from technical possibilities that have been developed outside the artistic field. Thus the preconditions for electronic music production were created by frequency research and the *Musikwollen* of the composers could use this technology for their own ends without having been involved in making it available from the beginning.

---

25 Ernst Mach, *The Analysis of Sensations and the Relation of the Physical to the Psychical* (Chicago / London: 1914), 89.

The methodological approach that contrasts technology and *Kunstwollen* is in accord with the way of thought that does not separate natural science and humanities from one another, because the influence of the natural sciences "penetrates all our relationships, our whole life; their thinking is thus decisive everywhere".[26] This approach explains the limited readiness and even the disregard for abstract reasoning. As the Vienna art historian Max Dwořák put it, philosophy "lost the conductor's role in the symphony of the sciences, which it occupied in times of doctrinaire methods of research, and if it at all wishes to justify its existence it must travel the same difficult path that the other exact sciences have long since taken".[27]

The resentment against aesthetic-philosophical speculation resulting from such a position is characteristic of the Viennese scientific tradition. There are traces of it in Sigmund Freud, who accused aesthetics of concealing the lack of success of its efforts "beneath a flood of resounding and empty words".[28]

The tendency to close the gulf between natural science and the humanities showed itself most strongly in the "physicalism" of the Vienna Circle around [Moritz] Schlick, [Rudolf] Carnap, [Otto] Neurath and others. The (legitimate or illegitimate) aversion of the Vienna Circle to philosophical speculation removed from empirical research was aphoristically expressed in Rudolf Carnap's dictum that metaphysicians were "musicians without musical ability".[29]

The attention concentrated on the *Kunstwollen* on the one hand and its technical preconditions on the other encouraged the application of "exact" methods. From the very beginning, where this related to the technological means of music there was no difficulty. However, it meant overcoming the aversion to a systematic recording of the technological preconditions. This reserve was certainly also based on the inhibition

---

26 Ernst Mach, *Die Geschichte und die Wurzel des Satzes von der Erhaltung der Arbeit* (Leipzig: 1909), 12 [*The History and the Root of the Principle of the Conservation of Energy*].
27 Quoted from Dagobert Frey, "Max Dwořáks Stellung in der Kunstgeschichte", in Kunsthistorisches Institut des Bundesdenkmalamtes (ed.), *Wiener Jahrbuch für Kunstgeschichte,* vol.I (XV) (Vienna: 1922), 14.
28 Sigmund Freud, *Civilization and its Discontents* (New York: 1962), 29–30.
29 Karl J. Brand, *Ästhetik und Kunstphilosophie im "Wiener Kreis"* (Essen: 1988), 92.

at applying all one's energy to questions that were frequently ascribed to the subordinate rank of ancillary sciences.

The fact that without answering the question of the technological preconditions of musical action some of the central problems of musicology cannot be overcome either has of course become understandable in recent times. The development of the electronic media threw up the challenge to turn attention to the possibilities that they opened up and also the limitations that they might set. This evolution of the 20th century also sharpened the view of the sociologists for the changes in general technological and legal-technological conditions. The concept of the "technological" has become so extended that it

a) includes the technologisation of music through the score in the same way as the technologising of the word through the alphabet is taken account of by linguistics;[30]

b) takes account of the changes in musical communication created by printed music;

c) takes account of the phonographic recording of music as a new element;

d) does not neglect the transformation of legal techniques as laid down in copyright law, ancillary copyright law and regulations of the functions of the collecting societies, and

e) includes the function of new communication technologies such as cable and satellite systems in the reckoning.

The number of monographies dealing with the influence of technological change of the above mentioned or similar kinds and seeking to estimate their significance for the impulse to music is constantly growing, as can be seen from the bibliographical overviews on music sociology.[31] The analysis of the technological mutations that are relevant for music

---

30 Walter J. Ong, *Orality and Literacy: The Technologizing of the Word* (London: 1988).

31 cf. Tibor Kneif, "Gegenwartsfragen der Musiksoziologie", *Acta Musciologica*, 38/1966, 72–118; J. Fukac / L. Mokry / V. Karbusicky, *Die Musiksoziologie in der Tschechoslowakei* (Prague: 1967); S. Micha Namenwirth / Karin Vander Linden, *Muziek en Maatschappij. Geannoteerde Basisbibliografie* (Brussels: 1982); Henrik Karlsson, *Forskning om dagens musiksamhälle. Kulturpolitisk forskning och utveckling*, no. 4, Statens kulturråd (Stockholm: 1982); Vladimir Karbusicky, "Gegenwartsprobleme der Musiksoziologie", *Acta Musicologica*, 58/1986, 35–91.

and the concept of "mediamorphosis"[32] gained from it are here only mentioned in passing as examples of the modus operandi that sought to follow the methodological orientations of Alois Riegl, Max Weber and Guido Adler. However, it is particularly worth mentioning that one of the first important attempts to understand mediamorphosis as a process of the technological change in the music of our century was undertaken by Ernst Krenek, whose *Bemerkungen zur Rundfunkmusik*[33] [Comments on Broadcasting Music] are part of the foundations of music sociology, particularly since they not only highlight the function transformation (that is also the change of the *Musikwollen*) through radio and gramophone records, but also predict the possibility of a mutation of the activity of the composer, which afterwards became realisable: the product of the composer's work – Krenek believed – would no longer exclusively be written scores but technologically produced music: "In this case, the script and the sound of the work would be identical; its 'original', now represented in the manuscript of the score, would coincide with the means of reproduction and the whole complex of 'interpretation' of the work of music would completely disappear."[34]

The productiveness of mathematical and scientific methods in the research and description of the technological preconditions of musical communication is clear, because how could it otherwise be possible to study and describe the conditions of the production of musical works, the electro-acoustic and room-acoustic preconditions of musical communication, the effects of musical action, the potential and the actual reach of technological communications systems, the music available through the media and its acceptance by the public, the change in behaviour of professional musicians and laypeople and so on and so forth.

In contrast, the benefit of the application of "exact" methods in the exploration of the *Kunstwollen* is not immediately obvious at first glance. If, however, one interprets the *Kunstwollen* or – as one could also say – the *Musikwollen* as the crystallisation of the musical behaviour that is noticeable in particular social constellations, then it becomes clear

32 Kurt Blaukopf, *Beethovens Erben in der Mediamorphose*, (Heiden: 1989).

33 Ernst Krenek, "Bemerkungen zur Rundfunkmusik", *Zeitschrift für Sozialforschung*, 7/1938, 148–165, quoted from Oskar Vegt / Dieter Prokop (eds.), *Kritische Kommunikationsforschung* (Munich: 1973), 47–65.

34 ibid., 65, footnote 3.

that these patterns of behaviour are accessible to empirical research. The field research of both ethnology and sociology is oriented on investigating such patterns of behaviour, and it thereby provides the elements determining the respective *Musikwollen*. This is true not only of the behaviour in making music and composing but also of listening behaviour. In connection with the analysis of change in musical practice it has been noted that listening behaviour is guided by the "will"[35] [*Wollen*] and that this was already noted by Ernst Kurth.[36] The consideration of the *Musikwollen* in the numerous attempts to analyse the socio-psychological function of 20th-century popular music and to identify its characteristic musical behaviour seemed to be urgent.[37] Without the field research methods developed by sociology and ethnology, and without statistical surveys and evaluations, the works that served this end would not have been possible. Recently this led to the succinct observation that: "Historic music sociology lacks any methodological tool suited to the research of the musical phenomena of popular music."[38] Such a verdict can only be made if one ignores the methodological ideas that Guido Adler maintained following the line of thought of the Vienna School of Art History and, as must be admitted, found greater resonance in sociology than in musicology.

The theoretical framework for the application of "strict" methods in historiography was established by the Viennese mathematician and science historiographer Edgar Zilsel (1891–1944). Zilsel turned the question of the application of scientific methods to humanities into a subject of investigation[39] and in his study on the emergence of the concept of the genius[40] undertook the attempt to make statements on historical development tendencies ("laws") using the statistical study of historical documents. Here he referred to the fact that physical "sci-

---

35   Irmgard Bontinck, "Comportement d'écoute et pratique musicale", in Henri Vanhulst / Malou Haine (eds.), *Musique et société* (Brussels: 1988), 237.

36   Ernst Kurth, *Romantische Harmonik und ihre Krise in Wagners "Tristan"* (Bern: 1920), 15.

37   Irmgard Bontinck (ed.), *New Patterns of Musical Behaviour of the Young Generation in Industrial Societies* (Vienna: 1974); Reinhard Flender / Hermann Rauhe, *Popmusik* (Darmstadt: 1989).

38   Reinhard Flender / Hermann Rauhe , *Popmusik*, op. cit., 1.

39   Edgar Zilsel, *Das Anwendungsproblem* (Leipzig: 1916).

40   Edgar Zilsel, *Die Entstehung des Geniebegriffes: Ein Beitrag zur Ideengeschichte der Antike und des Frühkapitalismus* (Tübingen: 1926).

ences of fact" [*Tatsachenwissenschaften*] – in the sense of Ernst Mach – also only gradually achieved the rank of "exact" sciences, as the history of the astronomy of fixed stars at the beginning of our century testifies. The precondition for this, however, is the ascertaining of factual material and its statistical evaluation.[41] It was entirely in this sense that he demanded a "statistical" history. This could neither linger over "masterworks" nor neglect the mass of the mediocre: "The question as to whether an artistic or theoretical work is the product of a genius or a bungler would not even enter its investigation. Certain components of these value concepts, however, could reappear in other and more objective shapes." [42]

This approach coincides with Guido Adler's, who drew attention to the medium and minor masters of composition, who "collect the building blocks for a new *Kunstwollen*",[43] and called for definitions of style "without evaluation of beauty and without theories of beauty".[44] Adler even explicitly recommended the application of statistical procedures as a "perfect tool" for style-critical definitions.[45] Most clearly – and completely in agreement with Edgar Zilsel's understanding – in 1924, in his essay on *The Viennese Classical School* Adler said on this question: "Previously, research concerned itself only with the investigation of individual masters and pointing out, as if in coincidence, the shared characteristics of the school and the artistic, technical relations between the individual masters. Almost no use was previously made of the most important methodological means, statistical compilation. Methodological research itself is in a state of constant progress. And thus, after the analysis, the synthesis can intervene with greater certainty. As a result, it will be possible to substantiate and justify precisely some intuitive understandings in the literature and to show up some errors."[46] Adler's recommended route from the ascertaining of facts through the "intuitive understanding" of connections to "exact" foundation has – in this

---

41 ibid., 322.
42 Edgar Zilsel, *The Social Origins of Modern Science* (Dordrecht/ Boston/ London: 2000), 204.
43 Guido Adler, *Methode der Musikgeschichte*, op. cit., 143.
44 ibid., 122.
45 ibid., 34.
46 Guido Adler, "Die Wiener klassische Schule", in id. (ed.), *Handbuch der Musikgeschichte* (Tutzing: 1961), 793.

way at least – only in exceptional cases been consistently taken in musicology. It has been pursued with more energy by some sociologists, for example in the statistical recording of changes in "musical taste" on the basis of repertoire analyses,[47] which show concretely that the *Kunstwollen* of an epoch is not only determined by its own art, "but also by its relationship to every other one".[48] As the founder of music statistics emphasised, inquiries of this kind can not only serve to illuminate the epochal *Kunstwollen,* but also the apprehension of personal styles, because from the comparison of two or more complete bodies of works "one can retrospectively come to a comparison of the essential forms, that is, the personalities".[49]

New mathematical methods can also be of use in the investigation of historical changes in the *Musikwollen*. Thus the information-theory analysis of scores from the 10th and 11th centuries provided more precise details on the transition from musical chronicling to composition, by identifying the criteria of writing techniques for differentiating the descriptive memory notation from the prescriptive composition notation.[50] Undertakings of this kind also provide conclusions on the change of the *Kunstwollen,* which thereby proves to be accessible to scientific analysis. The fact that this kind of procedure is included in the sociology of music seems to us theoretically hardly justifiable, and is possibly only explicable from the fact that music sociology, as it were vicariously, incorporates those aspects and methods that have long only exceptionally been taken into consideration by music-history research.

The establishment of music sociology as a discipline is in no way owing to a need for autonomy. On the contrary, its roots go back to the thinking on the history of music and art at the turn of the century [that is around 1900]. What they were able to gain from the Vienna schools of art history and musicology and from the works by Ernst Mach on

47   John H. Mueller, *The American Symphony Orchestra* (Bloomington: 1951); id., *Fragen des musikalischen Geschmacks* (Cologne: 1963); Desmond Mark, *Zur Bestandaufnahme des Wiener Orchesterrepertoires* (Vienna: 1979); id., *John H. Mueller – ein Pionier der Musiksoziologie*, series "Musik und Gesellschaft" vol. 19 (Vienna: 1985).

48   Hans Tietze, *Methode der Kunstgeschichte*, op. cit., 175.

49   Leo Wilzin, *Musikstatistik: Logik und Methodik gesellschaftsstatistischer Musikforschung* (Vienna: 1937), 32.

50   Christian Kaden, *Musiksoziologie* (Berlin: 1984), 356ff.

the philosophy of science, has been further stimulated by the efforts to bridge the gap between the natural sciences and the humanities, i.e. through the works of Edgar Zilsel and the ideas of a "unified science" as put forward by the Vienna Circle. In contrast to the music sociology of Adorno and some other outstanding representatives of this discipline, this tradition is distinguished less by philosophical lustre than by empirical toil.

The Sociology of Art in the Orchestra of the Sciences[1]

That is, a sociology not just of people but also of things![2]

The definition of a scientific discipline and its demarcation from other disciplines is often regarded as an imperative. I would like to show that in the history of Austrian "sciences of the arts" [*Kunstwissenschaften*][3] the commitment to fluid boundaries and the effort to link different specialist disciplines has its tradition; that significant findings are owed to this style of thinking; that this way of thinking has experienced strengthening and precision through the logical empiricism of the Vienna Circle; and that it has also had consequences for the sociology of the arts.

Restrictive and integrative art sociologies

Two tendencies can be distinguished with regard to the position of art in the field of work of art sociology. One, which I would call *restrictive*, represents the belief that the sociology of art deals only with society and not with the arts. Art sociology is simply concerned with the social

---

1   Editorial note: first published in Alfred Smudits / Helmut Staubmann (eds.), *Kunst Geschichte Soziologie: Beiträge zur soziologischen Kunstbetrachtung aus Österreich: Festschrift für Gerhard Kapner* (Frankfurt am Main: 1997), 21–32.

2   Gerhardt Kapner, "Nachdenkliches zur Kunstsoziologie", in Irmgard Bontinck (ed.), *Kulturpolitik, Kunst, Musik: Fragen an die Soziologie*, series "Musik und Gesellschaft" vol. 22 (Vienna: 1992).

3   Editorial note: *Kunstwissenschaften* can literally be translated as "sciences of the arts". In the German-speaking academic world the term is often understood as a collective description for disciplines such as visual art, music and theatre, that is, "studies of the arts". A second terminological meaning points to an understanding of art history as a systematic discipline that includes a broad spectrum of topics and research questions. Both variants in meaning occur in Blaukopf's texts. Sometimes he uses *Kunstwissenschaften* in direct connection with *Musikwissenschaften* (*Kunst- und Musikwissenschaften*) and thus means "studies of the arts". Elsewhere it refers explicitly to the Vienna School, and here the second meaning applies, that is, "sciences of the arts". Rarely, *Kunstwissenschaften* is also used as a synonym for art history. We have taken account of this ambiguity in the translation and use one or the other translation depending on the context.

interweaving of the arts, says Alphons Silbermann, and not with "analyses of the art work itself".[4] In a similar sense, Fabio Dasilva insists that music sociology does not deal with music but with society.[5] In contrast, however, as a French sociologist notes, an art sociology that restricted itself to the investigation of the social factors of production, distribution and appreciation of music would remain a "poor relation" of the art sociologies that do not set themselves such barriers.[6]

The second tendency, which for want of a better term one could call *integrative*, rejects the restrictive concept of an art sociology that only deals with the people who have to do with art. It demands the attack on the thing itself,[7] "because society also sediments itself in the thing we are talking about, that is, in art, and therefore this, too, is an object of sociological study".[8]

Indeed, such differing thinkers as Max Weber and Theodor W. Adorno have followed this maxim – even if in their own different ways. The attempt to obey it, however, raises methodological questions that have by no means been treated exhaustively in the literature of art sociology. I am indebted to Gerhardt Kapner for the impulse to give them some thought.

Encyclopaedism

The widely acclaimed principle of interdisciplinarity, to which, however, often only lip service is paid, makes our research easier. This maxim, however, does not necessarily say how one should proceed. An answer to this question follows from the ideas of "logical empiricism", which were developed in the Vienna Circle since around 1930. In association with other representatives of this school of thought, Otto

---

4   Alphons Silbermann, *Empirische Kunstsoziologie* (Stuttgart: 1986), 46.
5   "For purposes of clarity, it should be understood that the sociology of music is thus not so much about music in itself as about society." Fabio Dasilva / Anthony Blasi / Dees David, *The Sociology of Music* (Indiana: 1984), vi.
6   See Antoine Hennion, *La Passion musicale: Une sociologie de la médiation* (Paris: 1993), 134.
7   Editorial note: the term "thing itself" (*die Sache selbst*) is here used in a phenomenological sense and not as a reference to a transcendental entity in Kant's sense (*das Ding an sich*).
8   Gerhardt Kapner, "Nachdenkliches zur Kunstsoziologie", in Irmgard Bontinck (ed.): *Kulturpolitik, Kunst, Musik: Fragen an die Soziologie*, series "Musik und Gesellschaft" vol. 22 (Vienna: 1992), 46.

Neurath (1882–1945) initiated the move for the "unity of science" and with his programme of encyclopaedism contributed to overcoming the artificial boundaries of the individual disciplines. In 1939 he wrote: "We should understand the social sciences as a collection of very many scientific units that can be combined in very different ways. This is real 'encyclopaedism' within the movement for the unity of science."[9]

The invitation to cooperation among the disciplines is conditional upon the agreement between their representatives: while the encyclopaedias were previously content with recommending their collaborators to treat every field with care and consideration, this new encyclopaedia was to bring its collaborators to agree with one another in order to push the unity of the form of research as far as possible.[10] The focus of this concept was thus on the communication between the disciplines.

The Call to Listen

It may be trivial to note this here especially, but it seems to me more than necessary to the situation: readiness to talk beyond the limits of the specialist discipline does not suffice for agreement between the disciplines. What results from this is simply the series of monologues that we know from some conferences and symposia. The will to listen is also needed. Only by acknowledging what the representatives of neighbouring disciplines know, can the exchange of words turn into the exchange of ideas. Otherwise it remains at the level of linguistic and conceptual confusion, as Otto Neurath showed in an essay on *Unified Science as an Empiricist Synthesis* (1938) based on the example of psychology: "If one reads the publications of the reflexologists, the psychoanalysts, the Gestalt psychologists, the behaviourists etc., one often does not know whether two researchers are speaking about the same thing in a different language or whether they are dealing with different things but are concerned with the same subject, or whether they agree on the facts and are just expressing themselves differently or whether their opinions are completely opposed to one another."[11]

---

9   Otto Neurath, *Gesammelte philosophische und methodologische Schriften,* vol. 2, edited by Rudolf Haller / Heine Rutte (Vienna: 1981), 899.
10 ibid., 721.
11 Otto Neurath, *Gesammelte philosophische und methodologische Schriften* 2, edited by Rudolf Haller / Heine Rutte (Vienna: 1981), 830.

In order to master such difficulties, encyclopaedism searches for a method of linguistic understanding between the disciplines. It is a question of finding a procedure according to which principles that arise in the most diverse specialist sciences can be connected with one another. Statements that arise in discussions about art, ethics or jurisprudence should be incorporated in a single language, a "universal jargon". Neurath was fully aware that in this way it could lead to a shifting of the usual boundaries of the disciplines. But, for him, the decisive benefit consisted in the construction of bridges between the sciences: "The fruitfulness of the unity of science movement is indicated by the fact that more and more students of special fields participate in the discussion of the relation of their discipline to other domains. In this way bridges between different fields are constructed at points where only isolated domains were found before."[12]

Neurath used a new term for this endeavour to stimulate communication between the disciplines, which became one of his favourite phrases: the orchestration of the sciences.

The Orchestration of the Sciences

Neurath did not coin this expression himself. It was used by the American Horace M. Kallen at the Fifth International Congress for the Unity of Science (Harvard, 1939). Neurath used this term as a technical instrument as well as to describe a democratic principle of the organisation of scientific research. "It is the problem of any democracy, which any actual scientific research organization has also to solve: on the one hand the nonconformists must have sufficient support; on the other hand, scientific research needs some cooperation. . . . What can we call this democracy of cooperation within the 'encyclopedism of logical empiricism'? I have no better word for that than Kallen's 'orchestration'."[13]

This term thus aims to serve encyclopaedism and the agreement between scientific domains. At the same time it arises from the "tolerant approach of democratic cooperation".[14]

---

12 Otto Neurath, "Unified Science and its Encyclopaedia", *Philosophy of Science*, vol. 4, no. 2, 1937, 271.
13 Otto, Neurath, "The Orchestration of Sciences by the Encyclopedism of Logical Empirism", *Philosophy and Phenomenological Research*, vol. 6, no. 4, 1946, 496–508.
14 ibid., 508.

Its underlying position, as Neurath expressly noted, is the tradition of Ernst Mach, in which he himself, the physician Philipp Frank, the mathematician Hans Hahn and the statistician Richard von Mises had been brought up.

The Relationship between the Natural and the Social Sciences

The attempt to orchestrate the sciences by no means extends merely to the natural sciences but pursues the attempt "to pass from chemistry to biology, from mechanics to sociology without altering the language applied to them".[15]

With Neurath himself, this need for a universal scientific language, a "universal jargon" as he said, was not directly triggered by natural-science considerations but precisely through his experience in socio-logical research. He disliked the so frequent reference in historical and sociological literature to vague terms such as *"Volksgeist"* [national spirit] or *"Herrschermentalität"* [ruler mentality]. He sought a method of talking about sociological and historical problems in a language that is similarly simple to that used by natural scientists in the laboratory. As an empiricist he asked himself how one could proceed from simple observational statements on which all further discussions could be built. This provided the impetus for Neurath, following Rudolf Carnap, to develop his ideas of "protocol sentences".[16]

In a retrospective essay written in 1945 Neurath expressly drew attention to this connection with sociology. The link between Neurath's sociological works of 1931 and his article on "protocol sentences" is also confirmed by the chronological sequence.[17] This may still be remarkable today, because it points to the logical connection of the effort to orchestrate sciences also between domains that are often still thought as being widely removed from one another, e.g. between sociology and physics.

---

15 ibid., 497.
16 Editorial note: "protocol sentences" are descriptive, empirically and logically founded propositions. Their status of being true or false results from an inter-subjective agreement.
17 Otto Neurath, *Empirische Soziologie: Der wissenschaftliche Gehalt der Geschichte und Nationalökonomie* (Vienna: 1931); Otto Neurath, "Soziologie im Physikalis-mus", *Erkenntnis*, 2/1931, 393–431; Otto Neurath, "Protokollsätze", *Erkenntnis*, 3/1932/33, 204–214.

In the sciences that deal with the arts the concept of interdisciplinarity continually gained ground. The transition from a predominantly philosophical aesthetics to empirically oriented "sciences of the individual arts" accelerated this process. In the sciences of the arts of the 19th century the crossing of the boundaries to social-science was virtually celebrated as an achievement. We can speak of a "sociologisation of sciences of the arts", which deserves our attention because it not only touches on the relationship of art history to the sociologies but also the relationship of the sociologies to the arts themselves.

The "Sociologisation" of the Sciences of the Arts

This process, which began in earnest in the 19th century and was essentially guided by considerations of a positivist philosophy, can be illustrated by several examples.

Austrian sciences of the arts undertook the step to the extension of the subject's boundaries in a radical-practical way and without any very detailed programmatic declarations. Thus Rudolf von Eitelberger (1817–1885) ensured the institutionalised connection between art and industrial production by founding the Vienna Museum for Art and Industry; he concerned himself with the economic fate of Austrian arts and crafts[18] and he did not consider analysing state subsidy policy to be something beneath his dignity as an art historian.[19] Thus Eitelberger was already working on areas that some art sociologists today regard as virgin territory that they have just discovered. Moriz Thausing (1838–1884), who came to the University of Vienna in 1873, developed methodological ideas on the foundation of art history as a science. In his inaugural lecture he developed a research strategy that sought to replace the customary aesthetic-philosophical speculation with positivist relevance: "There is no soul, no mind, no feeling – and whatever the words may be – in an art work that would not be carried into it through visible, very concrete forms, and that therefore would also be visible, readable from it in the same clear and recognisable ways."[20]

---

18   Rudolf Eitelberger von Edelberg, *Die österreichische Kunst-Industrie und die heutige Weltlage* (Vienna: 1871).

19   Rudolf Eitelberger von Edelberg, *Bemerkungen über das österreichische Kunstbudget aus Anlaß des Staats-Voranschlages 1884* (Vienna: 1884).

20   Moriz Thausing, "Die Stellung der Kunstgeschichte als Wissenschaft: Aus einer Antrittsrede an der Wiener Universität im Oktober 1873", in Moriz Thausing,

Thausing's pupil Alois Riegl (1858–1905) professed a similar under-standing and moreover expressly a "positivistic" method. He has with some right been described as "one of the first sociologists of art".[21] The term *Kunstwollen*,[22] which Riegl coined, has frequently been vaguely misunderstood. As Riegl's pupil Hans Tietze (1880–1954) emphasised, however, *Kunstwollen* is not a question of a mystic force, "but solely a concept that has been gained from the works and other utterances".[23] The fact that this empirically developed sociological category aroused Max Weber's interest is thus completely understandable.

In 1885 Guido Adler (1855–1941) described his methods of *musicology*, of which he is considered to be the founder. Simply the fact that in the process he clearly followed the ideas of the art historian Moriz Thausing identifies him as someone who goes beyond the boundaries of his sub-ject – as does his methodological adoption of the teaching of the physi-cist-philosopher Ernst Mach. Adler's part in the "sociologisation" of his discipline is confirmed by his thesis that the total culture, the climate and the economy represent factors "the influences of which on the develop-ment of art cannot be overlooked".[24] In his inaugural lecture in Vienna in 1898 he even gave research the task of "winding up the connecting threads" that lead from music to social, economic and political condi-tions.[25] Adler also adopted the sociological category of *Kunstwollen* from the Riegl pupil Hans Tietze, although not unconditionally.[26]

Richard Wallaschek (1860–1917) built a bridge between ethnology and musicology. Pure art-history researches, he believed, "no longer close themselves to the extension of their field through ethnology".[27] Simi-lar tendencies to crossing the boundaries of the subject and observing

---

Wiener Kunstbriefe (Leipzig: 1884), 19.

21 Paul Wimmer, "Ein vergessener Österreicher – der Kunsthistoriker Alois Riegl", *Österreichische Akademische Blätter*, 2/1967, 43.

22 Alois Riegl, *Problems of Style: Foundations for a History of Ornament* (Princeton: 1992).

23 Hans Tietze, *Methode der Kunstgeschichte* (Leipzig: 1913), 14.

24 Guido Adler, Umfang Methode und Ziel der Musikwissenschaft, *Vierteljahrs-schrift für Musikwissenschaft*, vol. 1, 1885, 12.

25 Guido Adler, "Musik und Musikwissenschaft", *Jahrbuch der Musikbibliothek Pe-ters für das Jahr 1898* (Leipzig: 1899), 35.

26 Guido Adler, *Methode der Musikgeschichte* (Leipzig: 1919), 10.

27 Richard Wallaschek, *Anfänge der Tonkunst* (Leipzig: 1903), 111.

positivist principles can also be seen in *literary studies*.[28] In his analysis of Middle Ages theatre, Richard Heinzel (1839–1905) did not content himself with the examination of the texts, but from them sought to reconstitute the step-by-step deepening of perception by the "audience". This "communications-science" approach, as we would put it today, was intended to reveal the process "that leads to the full understanding of what is portrayed and the corresponding aesthetic enjoyment".

For the German literature scholar Wilhelm Scherer (1841–1886) interdisciplinary empiricism was a methodological principle: "In his inclination to the strictest empirical-inductive methods, Scherer wanted at the same time to be a universal scholar who sought to call to mind the findings of music and art history, of theology and of social and political history and to make them useful for literary history in his way."[29] In his *Poetik* [orig. 1888], Wilhelm Scherer even concerned himself with the "exchange value of poetry and with literary intercourse". The value of poetry, Scherer explained, "regulates itself by supply and demand according to the relations of production and consumption. Recently this relationship has acquired a particular expression inasmuch as it concerns the literary product as a bare commodity. Since the 15th century at least, there has been a book trade in Germany, which then boomed as a result of the ease of production; the book trade brought about the recognition of poetry as a commodity."[30]

The fruitfulness of the integrative concept

These examples demonstrate that important Austrian art researchers of the 19th century were turning their attention to the neighbouring disciplines and above all expected better and more thorough conclusions about the arts themselves from the incorporation of what we today call the "social facts". Their methods were aimed at the transition from a "restrictive" concept of the discipline to an "integrative" one.

---

28 See Herta Blaukopf, "Positivismus und Ideologie in der Germanistik: Aus den Anfängen der österreichischen Sprach- und Literaturforschung", in Kurt Blaukopf (ed.), *Philosophie, Literatur und Musik im Orchester der Wissenschaften*, series "Wissenschaftliche Weltauffassung und Kunst" vol. 2 (Vienna: 1996).

29 Werner Richter / Eberhard Lämmert, "Einführung", in Wilhelm Scherer / Erich Schmidt, *Wilhelm Scherer, Erich Schmidt: Briefwechsel*, edited by Werner Richter (Berlin: 1963), 21.

30 Quoted from Gunter Reiss, "Einleitung", in Wilhelm Scherer, *Poetik: mit einer Einleitung und Materialien zur Rezeptionsanalyse* (Tübingen: 1977), 85.

I am by no means overlooking the fact that this integrative tendency was certainly not limited to Austria, even though it assumed particular force in this country. In his early years the great German historian Georg Gervinus (1805–1871) had already polemicised against authors who characterised a poet in a "makeshift" manner just based on his self while forgetting "that in history everything is connected",[31] and in the process he even developed a programme of sociological research for the purposes of literary history: "We completely lack a constructive summary of external means of promotion of poetic culture in the last century, of scholarly institutes, societies, princely patrons and protectors, of the book trade and the adoption of academics; and what a broad field for the most beautiful elucidations would a systematically ordered literary statistics that . . . offered convenient overviews open up."[32]

The forceful efforts of art historians to approach sociological questions in the *interests of art research* thus seems to be documented. In view of this historical experience, how could one explain or even justify an encapsulation of sociologies concerned with the arts from the arts themselves?

The Possible Legitimacy of Drawing Boundaries

There may be a possible legitimate motive for this if one puts forward the fact that the sociologies today have numerous procedures available that can be successfully applied in closely defined problem fields even without particular concern for the specific nature of the individual arts. For example, if questions of the dissemination, promotion and appreciation of art products are investigated on the basis of usefulness and during a particular phase of research without consideration of the particular characteristics of these art products. The specific instruments of sociological work might – for a short time – make such a separation from the "thing itself" ["*die Sache selbst*", that is, the concrete object of scientific research] useful or even necessary.

The decision for such a "restrictive" strategy might also make sense in the short term. The overall context, however, makes it impossible to avoid returning to the "integrative" concept developed by art history.

---

31 Georg Gervinus, "Schriften zur Literatur" (orig. 1833), in Edgar Marsch (ed.), *Über Literaturgeschichtsschreibung: Die historisierende Methode des 19. Jahrhunderts in Programm und Kritik* (Darmstadt: 1986), 135.
32 ibid., 135f.

In a long-term perspective, art sociology would have to become a science of the thing itself, i.e. deal with the arts. Precisely the fact that arts sediment themselves in social processes makes this unavoidable. For this reason Adorno flatly rejected a "non-musical music sociology": "Sociological concepts that are imposed on music from the outside, without being able to demonstrate their credentials in strictly musical terms, remain devoid of force."[33]

The process that Adorno complained about, of so to say imposing finished sociological concepts on a particular art form, is based on the residue of a metaphysical understanding: works of art are seen as independent, as images removed from all social compulsions, which are only to be put in their social context by sociologists. Art sociology would be able to do away with this ideological fossil if it defined the object of its research not as "art" but as a social process to which this "art" belongs.

"Art Praxis" as an Object of Research

A proposal emerges from the Vienna Circle which, if followed, is suited to dealing both with getting round the sublime aesthetic concept of "art" as much as with the habit of imposing theoretical concepts on this "art" as it were from outside. The author of this idea is Richard von Mises (1883–1953), known as a technician and mathematician (also incidentally as a Rilke scholar).

Von Mises' *Positivism: A Study of Human Understanding*, written in Turkish exile, was published by Otto Neurath in the Netherlands in 1939. The ideas that Mises develops in it coincide to a great extent with the basic ideas of the Vienna Circle. However, they differ from these ideas among other things through the more detailed statements on art and art history, which are worth noting.

Mises is of the view that it is not "art" that should form the object of scientific research but social practice in dealing with the arts, which he called *Kunstübung* [literally "art practice"]. The object of research is thereby described in such a way as to leave wide room for the traditional art histories as much as for the art sociologies. Mises described the task of art history in this sense: "Based upon geographic historical points of view, it [the science of arts] will seek to describe and to

33 Theodor W. Adorno, *Sound Figures* (Stanford: 1999), 2.

classify the observable phenomena in the area of art practice and to comprehend their connections with other facts of the individual and social life (as part of psychology and sociology)."[34]

Kunstübung, the term von Mises chose, can give rise to methodological benefits that deserve closer consideration.

One advantage is that the sociologisation of the sciences of the arts [*Kunstwissenschaften*] is not understood as the crossing of the disciplinary boundary, but as one of the tasks of the sciences of the arts itself. The historical process of this sociologisation in the sense presented here is so to speak legitimised retrospectively and expressly. Sociology (and psychology) is itself accorded a place in art-historical thought. The sociologists do not approach the arts so to speak from outside, in order to treat it with their methods, but find their legitimate area of work within the sciences of the arts itself.

The objects of the sciences of the arts therefore are not for example just the artworks, their characteristics and their history, but art praxis. As art praxis we understand *all social activity that has to do with art*. This includes:

a)   The creation of artworks that are complete in themselves and require no further specific artistic activity for their social existence (e.g. paintings, sculptures, synthetic-electronic music).

b)   The creation of artworks that may be understood as complete in themselves in the modern copyright sense but whose social effect still requires the realisation through "performance" (e.g. musical and dramatic works).[35]

c)   The creation of artworks that cannot conclusively be categorised under a) and b) or which may fall alternately into one or the other category (e.g. poems and plays that can be read as well as recited or performed).

d)   The creation of artworks that require a technical procedure to be socially effective (e.g. film, compact disc).

---

34   Richard von Mises, *Positivism: A Study in Human Understanding* (New York: 1956), 312.

35   "Many art works exist in the form of directions to others telling them what to do to actualize the work on a particular occasion. The directions may consist of a musical score, the script of a play, a manuscript to be printed, or plans for a building" (Howard S. Becker, *Art Worlds* (Berkeley: 1982), 210f.).

e) The different technical procedures of art and their psychological aspects associated with the process of creation.

f) The institutional, technical and economic preconditions for art to become socially effective (e.g. museums, theatres, radio, TV, concert halls, orchestras). These also include the performing practices of the "performing arts" listed under b).

This by no means completely describes the field of artistic praxis, as all aspects of the dissemination and appreciation of the arts as well as their repercussions on the creative process itself are also part of it. The reader will be able to complete the (incomplete) overview by themselves. For me it is here solely a question of establishing the diversity of the issues within the meaning of von Mises' definition of sciences of the arts. Above and beyond this, there are naturally numerous further tasks for the sociologies of art: overcoming the linguistic difficulties that arise from interdisciplinary processes; the logical question of the "compatibility" of specialist terminologies and the establishment of rules according to which, from the analysis of the individual arts, conclusions can be derived on "art in general". But that is another story.

On Kurt Blaukopf

Michael Parzer
Biographical Notes on Kurt Blaukopf 1914–1999

Kurt Blaukopf was born on 15 February 1914 in Czernowitz [Chernivt-si], Bukowina. After primary and secondary school in Vienna, at his father's wish he started a degree course in jurisprudence and political science at the University of Vienna. Even in the early 1930s, however, his real preference was for a scientific understanding of music.

The following is intended to outline Kurt Blaukopf's academic career, with particular attention to his writings. The division into six creative periods corresponds to the emphasis of their content. At the same time, these periods reflect the important stages of Blaukopf's academic career and above and beyond that form the basis of the chronological criteria for the arrangement of the Kurt Blaukopf Archive at the Institute for Music Sociology at the Vienna University of Music and Performing Arts.

1935–1947: Vienna, Paris, Jerusalem[1]

Blaukopf's first years as a student are marked by intense autodidactic study of music sociology. Looking back, Blaukopf described these auto-didactic ambitions as follows: "I spent every free minute in the music collection of the National Library in order to excerpt and comment on musicological literature, and I used the evenings in the extraordinarily extensive library of the Vienna Chamber of Workers primarily to gain a picture of the state of sociological research."[2]

Under the pseudonym "Hans E. Wind", in 1935 Blaukopf published his first essay, entitled "Die Endkrise der bürgerlichen Musik und die Rolle Arnold Schönbergs" [The Final Crisis of Bourgeois Music and the Role of Arnold Schönberg].[3] This, which even attracted the critical

---

1   Extensive documentation of this period of Blaukopf's work can be found in his autobiography *Unterwegs zur Musiksoziologie: Auf der Suche nach Heimat und Standort* (Graz / Vienna: 1998); cf. Herta Blaukopf, "Kurt Blaukopfs (musikalisches) Österreich-Verständnis", *Austriaca*, 56/2003, 131–145.
2   Kurt Blaukopf, *Unterwegs zur Musiksoziologie*, op. cit., 15f.
3   Hans E. Wind, *Die Endkrise der bürgerlichen Musik und die Rolle Arnold Schönbergs* (Vienna: 1935).

attention of Ernst Krenek and Theodor W. Adorno,[4] concerns a Marxist-influenced determination of the function of modern atonal music against the background of fundamental transformation processes in bourgeois society. Even if Blaukopf retrospectively described this essay as a "rash experiment",[5] its publication is of major significance with regard to his further ambitions in the academic sphere.

Hitler's seizure of power in Germany (1933) and the burgeoning Austro-fascism meant increasing insecurity and worry for the Jewish Blaukopf family. For this reason, Kurt's parents suggested he should take a several-month study visit to Paris. In this period he wrote numerous texts,[6] which already revolved around Blaukopf's central theme in music sociology: the sociology of the tonal systems. Back in Vienna, Blaukopf completed the manuscript of his "Music Sociology",[7] which, however, was only to be published twelve years later. In 1938 Blaukopf fled to Paris; he spent the years 1940 to 1947 in Jerusalem. In Paris his attention was drawn to the "aesthetics of the French Encyclopaedists"[8] and their influence on the philosophical intellectual history of Austria, a subject that accompanied him into his final years. At the forefront was the question of the special nature of Austrian music, which Blaukopf ascribed to the "intellectual and cultural peculiarity of Austria".[9] In his manuscript "Mozart: A Preface to the History of Austrian Music"[10]

---

4   cf. Ernst Krenek: "Eine soziologische Deutung der zeitgenössischen Musiksituation", *Wiener Zeitung*, 22 July 1935. In July 1935 Adorno wrote to Krenek: "Unfortunately (because of course one certainly wants a man who so openly admits to what one seeks oneself) I have to agree entirely with your critique of the Windian brochure. No, not like that, and in view of such consequences one can overcome the fear of one's own effectiveness." (Theodor W. Adorno / Ernst Krenek, *Briefwechsel* (Frankfurt am Main: 1974), 91).

5   Kurt Blaukopf, *Unterwegs zur Musiksoziologie*, op. cit., 16.

6   cf. for example Kurt Blaukopf, *Harmonie und Perspektive: Die Entwicklungsgeschichte der bürgerlichen Kunst* (unpublished manuscript, 1936/1938).

7   Kurt Blaukopf, *Musik und Gesellschaft: Bemerkungen über die Anwendung des historischen Materialismus auf die Musikgeschichte* (unpublished manuscript, 1938).

8   Kurt Blaukopf, *La Musique et les Encyclopédistes* (unpublished manuscript, 1940/1941); id., *Studien zur Musikästhetik der Enzyklopädisten* (unpublished manuscript, 1942), published later under the title of "Die Enzyklopädisten und die Musik", in Kurt Blaukopf, *Unterwegs zur Musiksoziologie*, op.cit., 144–171.

9   Kurt Blaukopf, *Die Weltgeltung der österreichischen Musik*, (unpublished manuscript, Paris: 1939).

10 Kurt Blaukopf, *Mozart: Ein Vorwort zur Geschichte der österreichischen Musik*

Blaukopf described the intellectual climate of the age of Joseph II, from which Viennese Classicism emerged. This interest in the cultural and national identity of Austria brought him into contact with the Free Austria movement and the Austria Society in Palestine, and thereby to the bookseller and later publisher Willy Verkauf,[11] who as a sponsor, academic partner and friend was to assume an important role in Blaukopf's later life.

1948–1964: From Music Criticism to Music Sociology

After his return to Austria in 1947, Blaukopf made his living as a music and culture journalist. In regular contributions to the newspapers *Der Abend, St. Galler Tagblatt* and *Heute,* and in columns for the *Nebelspalter,* Blaukopf dealt with current musical life in Vienna as well as questions of musical practice. In contrast to many of his colleagues, Blaukopf recognised the potential of the gramophone record very early on,[12] as well as the need for an independent "record journalism", which he put into practice as the co-founder of the record magazine *Phono* (1954) and later as a co-worker on the *HiFi-Stereophonie* magazine. In parallel to his journalistic work, in his series "Bücher der Weltmusik" [Books on World Music] Blaukopf published a number of reference works on famous musicians, musical genres and gramophone recordings;[13] in addition he published journalistic-style books on various musical issues.[14]

(unpublished manuscript, Jerusalem: 1940), published later under the title "Musik im Geiste der Aufklärung: Mozart und die Eigenheit der österreichischen Kultur", in Kurt Blaukopf, *Unterwegs zur Musiksoziologie,* op.cit., 108–143.

11   Not until 1962 did Blaukopf learn that Willy Verkauf and the painter Andé Verlon were one and the same person) (Kurt Blaukopf, "V=V. Notizen über einen kommunikativen Maler", *Der Monat,* yr. 15, 1962, 94–96).

12   As early as 1953 Blaukopf believed that the gramophone record would "very soon prove to be an important . . . pedagogical accessory". (Kurt Blaukopf, "Musik im Unterricht", *Musikerziehung,* 6/1953, 252).

13   cf. for example Kurt Blaukopf, *Lexikon der Symphonie* (Teufen / Bregenz / Vienna: 1952); id., *Grosse Dirigenten* (Teufen, 1953); id., *Grosse Virtuosen* (Teufen: 1954); id.: *Grosse Oper – Grosse Sänger* (Teufen: 1955); id., *Langspielplattenbuch: Konzert und Oper* (Vienna: 1956).

14   Kurt Blaukopf, *Hohes C zu vermieten: Nebi-Geräusche aus dem Musikleben der Gegenwart für lächelnde Leser* (Rorschach: 1956); id., *Hexenküche der Musik* (Teufen: 1957).

Alongside this, Blaukopf wrote scripts for radio broadcasts,[15] and in his biographical novel *Symphonie fantastique*,[16] published in 1959, he tried his hand as a novelist. Above and beyond this Blaukopf worked as a translator of several English-language works. This primarily bread-and-butter work in no way diminished his academic ambitions. In 1950, his music-sociology manuscript was published under the title "Music Sociology: An Introduction to Basic Concepts with Particular Attention to the Sociology of the Tonal Systems".[17]

As the first book in the German-speaking world with "music sociology" in its title, this study marked a milestone in the development of the sociology of the tonal systems, which had first been explained as an extensive field of research by Max Weber in his 1910 essay *The Rational and Sociological Foundations of Music*, which remained a fragment.[18] At the start of the study is the basic problem of the rational ordering of tones: the mathematical indivisibility of the octave into two equally large symmetrical parts. Against the view that the occidental tonal system was "logically correct" and therefore "culturally superior", which was widespread until the 20th century, Weber points out that there cannot be a "natural" system of tones that is practically applicable, but that each tonal system was the result of particular, more or less arbitrary conventions. Following Weber, Blaukopf argues for the "critical elimination of the fetishism that judges all music of past epochs according to the conventions of our 'equal, 12-step temperature'. This fetishism hinders a historical appreciation of the music of other eras and other peoples."[19] Above all, this absolutising of the occidental tonal system made it impossible to understand "the transformation processes that have been taking place in our music for decades".[20] The investigation of this transformation process, which took particular account of its

---

15 There are several hundred pages of radio scripts in the Blaukopf archives for the programmes *Aus der Hexenküche der Musik* (1958–1961) and *Jedes Ding hat zwei Seiten* (1958–1967).

16 Kurt Blaukopf, *Symphonie fantastique: Hector Berlioz: Leben, Liebe und Melodien eines romantischen Genies* (Teufen: 1959).

17 Kurt Blaukopf, *Musiksoziologie: Eine Einführung in die Grundbegriffe mit besonderer Berücksichtigung der Soziologie der Tonsysteme* (Vienna: 1950).

18 Max Weber, *The Rational and Sociological Foundations of Music* (Carbondale: 1958).

19 Kurt Blaukopf, *Musiksoziologie*, op.cit., 13.

20 ibid., 13.

contingency, was the main task of music sociology. This demand was thereby not directed only against a Eurocentric world view, but was also implicitly critical of the prevailing orientation towards an inherent musical aesthetic that predominated in the musicological discourse. Blaukopf emphasised the interplay of musical development and non-musical factors: "Here music sociology proceeds from the recognition that those social, political and economic conditions not only externally influence and colour the practice of music, but determine its innermost being."[21]

Around 1950 Blaukopf wrote a number of essays in which he gave a detailed explanation of the basic programme of this understanding of music sociology. Particularly noteworthy are "Musiksoziologie: Probleme und Aufgaben" [Music Sociology: Problems and Tasks],[22] published in 1949, and the article published three years later, "Musiksoziologie: Bindung und Freiheit bei der Wahl von Tonsystemen" [Music Sociology: Ties and Freedom in the Choice of Tonal Systems].[23] In the course of these considerations Blaukopf outlined his understanding of music sociology in increasingly clear contours. In his entry on music in the *Dictionary of Sociology* (1955) he formulated his pioneering definition of music sociology: "the compilation of all social data relevant to musical practice, the classification of this data according to its importance for musical practice, and the recording of data of crucial significance in altering practices."[24] In this period of his writing, against the

---

21 ibid., 14. In his "music sociology" Blaukopf oriented himself closely on Plekhanov's materialist theory of society, which later, however, significantly faded into the background in favour of a less orthodox interpretation of Marxism. For a critique of Blaukopf's "music sociology", see above all Kneif, *Musiksoziologie* (Cologne: 1971).

22 Kurt Blaukopf, "Musiksoziologie. Probleme und Aufgaben", *Europa-Archiv*, December 1949, 2651–2655.

23 Kurt Blaukopf, "Musiksoziologie – Bindung und Freiheit bei der Wahl von Tonsystemen", in Carl Brinkmann (ed.), *Soziologie und Leben: Die soziologische Dimension der Fachwissenschaften* (Tübingen: 1952), 237–257. In this context see also Blaukopf's analysis of the possibilities for the application of atonal music in compositional practice, Kurt Blaukopf, "Der Ton macht die Musik: Zur Soziologie von Tonalität und Atonalität", *Bücherschau*, yr. 3, vol. 3/4, 1949, 1; id., "Neue Beiträge zum Problem der Atonalität", *Österreichische Musikzeitschrift*, 6/1949, 140–142.

24 Kurt Blaukopf, "Musik", in Wilhelm Bernsdorf / Friedrich Bülow (eds.), *Wörterbuch der Soziologie* (Stuttgart: 1955), 342–346.

background of the growing dispute over the direction of music sociology, whose most prominent exponents in German speaking countries included Theodor W. Adorno and Alphons Silbermann,[25] Blaukopf endeavoured to establish the position of his music sociology research, about which he had long since provided information in his largely unnoticed article "Was ist Musiksoziologie?" [What is Music Sociology][26] and an essay on concert-hall acoustics.[27]

Blaukopf has the investigation of the influence of concert-hall acoustics on music[28] to thank for his personal acquaintance with Theodor W. Adorno, who was significantly to influence his further academic career. Adorno wrote to Blaukopf concerning his "Music Sociology" and the 1960 essay in the *Gravesaner Blättern* "Raumakustische Probleme der Musiksoziologie" [Concert-Hall-Acoustic Problems of Music Sociology]: "You cannot know how precisely both of these hit my current work: in the coming term I am holding a lecture to be followed by a discussion on music sociology. I have just had the thought of whether you would be able to come to Frankfurt and give a lecture and take the following seminar?"[29] Blaukopf's guest lecture in Frankfurt on 6 February 1962 evoked great interest.[30] At the end of the year he received a

---

25 cf. Theodor W. Adorno, "Ideen zur Musiksoziologie", in Theodor W. Adorno, *Klangfiguren – Musikalische Schriften I* (Berlin / Frankfurt am Main: 1959), 9–31; id., "Thesen über Kunstsoziologie", *Kölner Zeitschrift für Soziologie und Sozialpsychologie*, yr. 19, 1967, 87–93; Alphons Silbermann, "Die Stellung der Musiksoziologie innerhalb der Soziologie und der Musikwissenschaft", *Kölner Zeitschrift für Soziologie und Sozialpsychologie*, yr. 10, 1958, 102–115; id., "Anmerkungen zur Musiksoziologie: Eine Antwort auf Theodor W. Adornos 'Thesen zur Kunstsoziologie'", *Kölner Zeitschrift für Soziologie und Sozialpsychologie*, yr. 19, 1967, 538–545.

26 Kurt Blaukopf, "Was ist Musiksoziologie? Über Kinderkrankheiten einer jungen Wissenschaft", *phono*, yr. 7, vol. 1, 1960, 4–7.

27 Kurt Blaukopf, "Raumakustische Probleme der Musiksoziologie", *Gravesaner Blätter*, 5/1960, 163–173.

28 cf. for example, Kurt Blaukopf, "Über die Veränderung der Hörgewohnheit: Aktuelle Bemerkungen zum akustisch-technischen Einfluss auf den musikalischen Geschmack", *Schweizerische Musikzeitung*, yr. 94, vol. 2, 1954, 60f.; id., "Der Raum macht die Musik: Anmerkungen zur Beziehung von Raumakustik und Klangideal", *Musica*, yr. 14, vol. 8, 1960, 480–483.

29 Adorno to Blaukopf, letter of 27 September 1961.

30 Thus in his introduction to music sociology Adorno writes that Blaukopf had opened up "highly productive perspectives on the relationship between

teaching position in music sociology at the Vienna Academy of Music (today the University of Music and Performing Art).

1965–1976: Music Sociology, Music Pedagogics and Gustav Mahler

In September 1965 the Institute for Music Pedagogical Research was founded. The following years marked a turning point in Blaukopf's work: as a result of the security of the institute – in 1968 Blaukopf became a university professor of music sociology at the Vienna Academy of Music, in 1974 an honorary professor at the University of Vienna – he could then concentrate fully on his research work. Alongside his explicit music sociology research, Blaukopf gave more attention to cultural and media policy issues: in 1969 he founded the Institute for Music, Dance and Theatre in the Audio-Visual Media (IMDT); from 1972 to 1976 he was the first Austrian to sit on the executive committee of Unesco. The following years were marked by intense academic productivity as well as a lot of travelling. The diversity of his research themes in this period of work is notable: the spectrum ranged from rock bands to Gustav Mahler. While the tasks of music sociology were being more specifically defined at the theoretical level, Blaukopf increasingly turned to applied research. Through his connection with the Academy for Music and Performing Art, the focus increasingly centred on music-pedagogical questions.[31] The observation of the increasing gulf between teaching content and the "new sound experience of the young generation" prompted a broad research project. Blaukopf formulated the tasks of the new institute as follows: "The Music Pedagogical Research Institute sets itself the main aim of drafting a comprehensive textbook which takes the 'knowledge of the students' into consideration . . . and above and beyond this also takes account of the sociological change in the relationship to music in a technological age. . . .

---

acoustics and music sociology." (Theodor W. Adorno, *Einleitung in die Musiksoziologie* (Frankfurt am Main: 1962), 11). The manuscript of the lecture was published in the same year: Kurt Blaukopf, "Raumakustische Probleme der Musiksoziologie", *Die Musikforschung*, yr. 15, 1962, 237–246.

31   For texts about Blaukopf's music pedagogy, see for example: Franz Niermann, "...was 'erhältlich' ist: Musiksoziologische Anregungen für den Unterricht", *Musikerziehung*, yr. 53, 2000, 134–137; K. Peter Etzkorn, "Music and its Audience: Reflections on Blaukopf's Sociology and Implications for Music Education in the United States", *Musikerziehung*, yr. 53, 2000, 137–147.

The methodologically primary, but practically equal second main aim of the course as the sum of the sound experiences of the young generation results from this. Both tasks are tackled in parallel, so that the guidelines for the drafting of a new textbook can be derived from the respective level of the research work."[32]

This parallel pursuit of fundamental research and applied research characterises Blaukopf's typical style of work, which he would continue in the following decades. His commitment to cultural and educational policy issues was constantly based on an associated empirical analysis of the phenomena that were up for debate, the results of which then formed the main basis for policy decisions.

What, however, did Blaukopf understand by the "sound experiences of the young generation"? The establishment of new technological innovations, above all records and electro-acoustic sound production, had massively changed the world of sound. Blaukopf raised the question of the consequences these changes had for the perception, behaviour, and the subject itself – music. His largely unbiased approach, which distinguished him from often very culturally pessimistic contemporaries, is striking. Blaukopf appealed for the investigation of the "acoustic experience" of young people "without any preconceived aesthetic judgement".[33]

Against the background of rapid technological development, the question of the effect on these new technologies became increasingly controversial – both for music teachers as well as for cultural policy decision-makers. Founded in February 1969, the IDMT (International Institute for Music, Dance and Theatre in the Audio-Visual Media, from 1976 Mediacult), which Kurt Blaukopf headed until 1989, dedicated itself to the relationship between technology and art. The institute's task is the creation of teaching programmes, the organisation of experimental workshops, and above all the research into qualitative changes in the creation of culture through the technical media in the context of production, distribution and consumption.[34]

---

32 Kurt Blaukopf, "Musikpädagogisches Forschungsinstitut", *Musikerziehung*, yr. 19, 1965/66, no. 5, 1966, 203–207.

33 Kurt Blaukopf, "Probleme der klanglichen Erfahrung der jungen Generation", *Musik und Unterricht*, 1968, 241.

34 Kurt Blaukopf, "Die qualitative Veränderung musikalischer Mitteilung in den technischen Medien der Massenkommunikation", *Kölner Zeitschrift für Soziolo-*

The institute's first major project dealt with the "new musical behaviour of the young generation": starting from the results of music teaching research in the previous years, this project focused on the investigation of the new technical media on young people's musical activity. The rise of beat and rock bands represented a thus far unresearched phenomenon, in the face of which many music teachers were often helpless and uncertain.

In the framework of a five-year Unesco project with the cooperation of international institutes and experts, the attempt was made to answer the question of the cultural significance of these new forms of behaviour.[35] Contrary to pessimistic assumptions according to which the advance of technologically mediated music would lead to the "death of live music", the IMDT investigation showed an increase in musical independence, which was above all evident in the form of youth music groups. In this connection, Kurt Blaukopf carried out pioneering work in the research of young people's amateur rock bands: he studied some of these bands' main characteristics, which included electro-acoustic instruments as well as subcultural identity, which were subsequently studied as a "critique of established culture".[36] Further music sociology issues that Blaukopf analysed in the 1970s included audience research,[37] the structural analysis of musical life[38] and a concern with light music.[39]

---

gie und Sozialpsychologie, yr. 21, no. 3, 1969 , 510–516; id., "Musical Institutions in a Changing World", *International Review of the Aesthetics and Sociology of Music*, vol. 3, no. 1, 1972, 35–42.

35 cf. Kurt Blaukopf, "Pop, Beat and Rock: Doing your Electrical Thing", *Unesco Features*, no. 651, 1973; id., "New Patterns of Musical Behaviour of the Young Generation in Industrial Societies", in Irmgard Bontinck (ed.), *New Patterns of Musical Behaviour: A Survey of Youth Activities in 18 Countries* (Vienna: 1974), 13–30; id., "The influence of electroacoustics on patterns of musical behaviour", *Psychology of Music*, vol. 2, 1974, 29–31; Kurt Blaukopf / Irmgard Bontinck / Harald Gardos / Desmond Mark, *Kultur von unten: Innovationen und Barrieren in Österreich* (Vienna: 1983).

36 Irmgard Bontinck, *Kritik der etablierten Kultur* (Vienna: 1977); See also: Kurt Blaukopf / Irmgard Bontinck / Harald Gardos / Desmond Mark, *Kultur von unten: Innovationen und Barrieren in Österreich* (Vienna: 1983).

37 Kurt Blaukopf, *Musik und Publikum: Aktuelle Probleme der Musiksoziologie* (unpublished manuscript, 1973).

38 cf. for example Kurt Blaukopf, "Strukturanalyse des Musiklebens", *Musik und Bildung*, 1/1971, 11–15.

39 cf. for example Gunnar Sønstevold / Kurt Blaukopf, *Musik der 'einsamen Masse':*

Apart from the above-described sociological work – although by no means independent of it – from the late 1960s Blaukopf dedicated himself to the composer Gustav Mahler, and so to a theme that was to win him an international reputation far beyond the boundaries of the discipline: his biography of Mahler,[40] which was translated into eight languages, appeared in 1969. This book not only contained a wealth of material on the life and work of Gustav Mahler, but above and beyond this undertook the attempt at a fruitful combination of media-sociology and musicological research. Thus one of the book's central theses was that Mahler's music, which demanded a particular spatial sensitivity, could only be fully appreciated in an age in which technology would show its advantage: "The best stereo recordings of recent times can at last give us a sound image closer to Mahler's intentions than almost any concert performance. . . . Thanks to the techniques of electro-acoustic recording and reproduction, textual purity can be preserved and Mahler's original intention, as manifested in his notation, fulfilled."[41] Blaukopf's biography of Mahler is considered to have pointed the way for the work of the International Mahler Institute, founded in 1955; his further research on Mahler, which he partly carried out together with Herta Blaukopf, are of fundamental importance for the relatively late appreciation of Mahler.[42]

Alongside his academic work, Kurt Blaukopf continued to work as an important commentator on Austrian musical life: as a music critic he wrote for the *Nebelspalter* magazine (until 1975) and in 1965 he assumed the Vienna editorial of the record magazine *HiFi-Stereophonie* (until 1973). Above and beyond this Blaukopf acted as an adviser to the Vienna Festival and produced a large number of radio programmes.

Ein Beitrag zur Analyse von Schlagerschallplatten, series "Musik und Gesellschaft" vol. 4 (Karlsruhe: 1968); Kurt Blaukopf, "Künstlerische Ambitionen und Techniken in der leichten Musik", *Gravesaner Blätter*, 1/1956, 71–73.

40 Kurt Blaukopf, *Gustav Mahler* (New York: 1973) (original publication in German 1969).

41 ibid., 253

42 cf. for example Kurt Blaukopf, *Mahler: Sein Leben, sein Werk und seine Welt in zeitgenössischen Bildern und Texten* (Vienna: 1976); see also the extended revised edition: Kurt Blaukopf / Herta Blaukopf, *Gustav Mahler – Leben und Werk in Zeugnissen der Zeit* (Stuttgart: 1994); Herta Blaukopf (ed.), *Mahler / Unbekannte Briefe* (Vienna: 1983).

1977–1984: Technology, Media and Culture: Music in a Changing Society

In 1977 Kurt Blaukopf assumed the direction of the newly established – and until today Austria's only – chair of music sociology. The following seven years were marked by intensive travelling: Blaukopf gave lectures in Germany, France, Poland and the United States. In addition there were extensive expert and advisory activities and cooperation with the Commission for Music in Cultural, Educational and Mass Media Policies of the ISME (International Society for Music Education), founded on Blaukopf's suggestion in 1976. Some of the fundamental texts on music sociology were written in this period,[43] in which he increasingly dealt with methodological questions. In the unpublished manuscript "Patterns of musical behaviour on the contribution of sociology towards historical and cross-cultural research in the field of music",[44] based on a series of his research projects carried out in the 1960s and 1970s, he explicated the role of three fundamental epistemological principles of his music research. These include first an intercultural and historical comparative approach, second interdisciplinarity, and third value-free judgements. Blaukopf demanded the combination of the "observation of music in different cultural regions of our day with the analysis of historical stages in the European occidental development of music. ... While musicology usually limited itself to stating certain common features – such as a correspondence between the parallel fifths and fourths of the medieval organum and similar phenomena in Icelandic or Caucasian folk polyphony – the sociologist is trying to answer the question, whether such correspondence is generated by the societal context in which the music is made. The purely musical comparison is broadened to a cross-cultural comparison."[45]

The result of such an approach is a broad spectrum of different questions which, as he believed, an individual discipline was often not in

---

43 Kurt Blaukopf, "Sociology of Music: Sources and Functions of a New Science", *Austria Today* 1/1977, 28f.; id., "La Sociologie Musicale en Autriche", *Ex Austria: Cahiers universitaires d'information sur l'Autriche*, no. 5, 1977, 161–166.
44 Kurt Blaukopf, *Patterns of Musical Behaviour: On the contribution of sociology towards historical and cross-cultural research in the field of music* (unpublished manuscript in German and English, 1977).
45 ibid., 4.

a position to resolve. According to Blaukopf, musicology, communications research, psychology, psychoacoustics and biology should cooperate on an equal basis: "The new type of interdisciplinarity is remarkable for the fact that there is no longer one superior discipline and several auxiliary sciences that play a subordinate role, but that in the process of solving a problem, the various disciplines may alternatingly take the lead."[46]

In the end, Blaukopf appealed for the value-free social-science approach that Max Weber had already been calling for at the beginning of the 20th century. Sociology should in no way become a slave to the developments he described: "The loving care he [the sociologist] uses in the analysis of rock and beat, of musique concrète and aleatory (sic) experiments, of serial and post-serial music, ought not to be mistaken for love of this music. The taste and preferences of the sociologist have to be left out of consideration. He may even have misgivings and feel concern about such developments. But as long as he wishes to remain a sociologist he'd better not voice them. His must be Spinoza's proud motto: I do not condemn nor praise; I merely study."[47]

The book *Musik im Wandel der Gesellschaft* [Musical Life in a Changing Society],[48] whose international reception[49] made Blaukopf a representative of German-language music sociology far beyond the borders of his own country, was published in 1982. This work, which in the meantime has become a classic of music sociology, largely consists of the presentation of Blaukopf's music-sociology research areas, and on the other hand it offers a comprehensive overview of the history of music sociology. In the first and introductory chapter, above and beyond this Blaukopf undertook a theoretical and epistemological determination of the subject matter of his music sociology.[50]

---

46 ibid., 14.
47 ibid., 18.
48 Kurt Blaukopf, *Musik im Wandel der Gesellschaft: Grundzüge der Musiksoziologie* (Munich: 1982); id., *Musical Life in a Changing Society: Aspects of Music Sociology* (Portland: 1992).
49 Among the more than 60 reviews are statements by prominent representatives of music sociology such as Alphons Silbermann, Christian Kaden, Vladimir Karbusicky, Tibor Kneif, Carl Dahlhaus etc.
50 Kurt Blaukopf, "Ziele der Musiksoziologie", first chapter in id., *Musik im Wandel der Gesellschaft: Grundzüge der Musiksoziologie* (Munich: 1982), 15–22. Published

At the same time Blaukopf continued his research focus on the "mutation of musical life under the influence of technical media".[51] His texts on media and cultural policy were not only received with great interest by music professionals but also in the political world. His critical analysis of contemporary cultural and media policy, although far removed from culturally pessimistic laments, dealt with the question of the problems ensuing from the intersection of the mass media, economics and artistic creation and the consequences that should be drawn for the development of political measures.[52] The task of research, however, consisted only in preparing a possibility to assess existing or potential consequences: "i.e. categorising them on the basis of a cultural value system as "desired", "unwanted" or "natural". This categorisation is not the task of research. It is obliged solely to make data available that make the categorisation possible, i.e. preparing decision-making aids for cultural policy, media policy and legal policy etc."[53]

Further research works include a comprehensive project on the sociography of Austrian musical life,[54] research into the sound environment and the music of everyday life,[55] and a study carried out together with Willy Verkauf (André Verlon) on the influence of television on the popularisation of fine art.[56]

Blaukopf carried out pioneering work with his research on the record: his competence and familiarity with this medium through his long work with the record magazines *Phono* and *HiFi-Stereophonie* proved

---

also in this anthology, see page 13–20.

51 Kurt Blaukopf, *Die Mutation des Musiklebens unter dem Einfluss der technischen Medien* (unpublished manuscript, 1979).

52 Kurt Blaukopf, "Die Zukunft der darstellenden Künste und die Medien", *Musik und Bildung*, no. 2, 1977, 101–103; id., "Die Medien und die neue musikalische Realität", *Musik und Bildung*, no. 6, 1977, 326f.

53 Kurt Blaukopf, *Der Begriff des "cultural lag" in der "Mutationsforschung"* (unpublished manuscript, s.a.), 2.

54 The "sociography of musical life" was understood as a stocktaking of the most wide-ranging musical activities in a defined geographical area; cf. for example Kurt Blaukopf, "The Sociography of Musical Life in Industrialised Countries: A research task", *The World of Music*, vol. III, 1979, 78–86.

55 cf. for example Kurt Blaukopf, "Akustische Umwelt und Musik des Alltags", in Reinhold Brinkmann (ed.), *Musik im Alltag* (Mainz: 1980), 9–26.

56 Kurt Blaukopf / André Verlon, *Die Galerie: Das Verhältnis der TV-Berichterstattung zur Entwicklung der Kunstgalerien in Wien* (Vienna: 1980).

advantageous for the scientific concern with the significance of the new recording media. As early as 1977 the book *Massenmedium Schallplatte* [The Record as a Mass Medium][57] was published, in which Kurt Blaukopf above all analysed the sociocultural significance of the record against the background of methodological considerations on cultural statistics. This study formed the preparatory work for the interdisciplinary Mediacult project "The Phonogram in Cultural Communication",[58] which dealt with cultural, economic, legal and cultural-policy dimensions of the new recording medium.

Shortly before being made emeritus professor in 1984, Blaukopf together with the Vienna sociologist Wolfgang Schulz headed a research project on the social situation of composers in Austria,[59] whose findings led to a call for structural change in cultural policy: "The demand for an increase in the funding for artists is . . . not the deciding nor even the only factor that may be suited to improving the social situation of the artists. Far more important is the idea of a harmonisation of social policy, copyright policy, tax policy and media policy with declared aims of cultural policy."[60] With this demand Kurt Blaukopf marked a turning point in his research work: active commitment in cultural and media-policy affairs were to play a central role in the next five years.

1985–1990: Culture and Media Policy in Mediamorphosis

The years after Blaukopf was made emeritus professor are marked by intensive research activity as the head of the Mediacult institute and increased commitment in the field of cultural, media and education policy, which gave him an influential voice as a public commentator on Austrian and European cultural policy. With the "mediamorphosis" concept, formulated in 1989, Blaukopf developed a framework for the research into the processes and factors that are of key importance for musical practice at the end of the second millennium.

---

57 Kurt Blaukopf, *Massenmedium Schallplatte: Die Stellung des Tonträgers in der Kultursoziologie und Kulturstatistik* (Wiesbaden: 1977).

58 cf. for example Kurt Blaukopf (ed.), *The Phonogram in Cultural Communication: Report on a Research Project Untertaken by Mediacult* (Vienna / New York: 1982).

59 cf. Landeskulturreferentenkonferenz (ed.), *Künstler in Österreich* (Salzburg: 1984).

60 Kurt Blaukopf, "Die soziale Lage der Komponisten in Österreich", *Österreichische Musikzeitschrift*, yr. 39, vol. 10, 1984, 499.

In his essay "Die Stunde der Musik im Jahrzehnt der Medienexplosion" [The Hour of Music in the Decade of the Music Explosion],[61] published as early as 1985, Blaukopf emphasised that "as a result of the media explosion, music is gaining a new and presumably dominant position in people's lives"[62] and demanded that politics and pedagogics should finally take this fact into account. The implications associated with this media explosion are the main interest of the research project "Der Mensch in seiner Medienumwelt" [Man in His Media Environment],[63] which is considered to be an important preliminary work for the later works on mediamorphosis research. In the following, the development history of the programme, originally called "mutation research" is to be outlined.

As early as the first edition of his book *Musik im Wandel der Gesellschaft* (1982) Blaukopf used the term "mutation" in connection with the change in musical communication processes through technical media. This mutation includes the sum of changes that take place through the use of sound and image recorders, radio, film, cable and satellite systems. There is a detailed description of this term in the article "Cultural Mutation Brought on by New Technologies".[64] Following Georges Balandier, who made the originally biological term "mutation" fruitful for sociology,[65] Blaukopf named the following characteristics of cultural transformation processes through technical media: these changes are irreversible (1), have not taken place in a linear way but suddenly (2), take place in a disguised way – i.e., they are not immediately identifiable as such (3) and are extremely rapid (4). At the end of the 1980s Blaukopf replaced the word "mutation" with the term "mediamorphosis". According to Blaukopf, this word "is intended to sensitise us to the fact that mediamorphosis is a total process that includes all elements

---

61 Kurt Blaukopf, "Die Stunde der Musik im Jahrzehnt der Medienexplosion", in AGMÖ (ed.), *Musikerziehung in der Mediengesellschaft* (Eisenstadt: 1985), 15–24.

62 ibid., 15.

63 cf. for example Kurt Blaukopf, "Der Mensch in seiner Medienumwelt: Ein Beispiel für einen Programmschwerpunkt im Rahmen der Weltdekade", in Österreichische Unesco-Kommision (ed.), *Weltdekade für kulturelle Entwicklung (1988–1997)* (Vienna: 1987), 22–28.

64 Kurt Blaukopf, "Cultural Mutation Brought on by New Technologies", *Communications*, vol. 11, no. 3, 1985, 37–49.

65 Georges Balandier, "Sociologie des mutations", in id: *Sens et puissance. Les dynamiques sociales* (Paris: 1971).

of musical communication: artistic creation, the distribution of music, the appreciation of music, the occupational images of those working in this field, public funding, copyright law and – not least – media law".[66] In his book *Beethovens Erben in der Mediamorphose"* [Beethoven's Heirs in Mediamorphosis][67] Blaukopf described the three central elements of mediamorphosis: "1. The adaptation of the musical message to the technological conditions of recording and reproduction; 2. The use of technological possibilities in the interests of the musical message; 3. The changing of the reception of the musical message that is conditioned or facilitated by these elements."[68] Such a perspective focuses on the one hand on the level of production, distribution and reception of the totality of present-day musical practice; at the same time, however, it attempts to take account of the historical peculiarity of these transformation processes: "The concept of mediamorphosis . . . seeks to do justice to the real interconnections of all factors currently influencing music, and at the same time to bring out the particular elements of this present mutation."[69]

The research works resulting from this programme concerned themselves among other things with questions of cultural identity in the age of globalisation,[70] with the effects of new technologies on the creation of culture and the status of artists,[71] with copyright law and ancillary

66 Kurt Blaukopf, "Musik in der Mediamorphose: Plädoyer für eine kulturelle Marktwirtschaft", *Media Perspektiven*, 9/1989, 553. Here – even if with different aims – there are strong parallels to Richard A. Peterson's "production of culture" approach, which was developed independently of Blaukopf; see Richard A. Peterson, "Why 1955? Explaining the Advent of Rock Music", *Popular Music*, vol. 9, 1990, 97–116.

67 Kurt Blaukopf, *Beethovens Erben in der Mediamorphose: Kultur-und Medienpolitik für die elektronische Ära* (Heiden: 1989).

68 ibid., 5f.

69 Kurt Blaukopf, *Musical Life in a Changing Society: Aspects of Music Sociology*, op. cit., 248. For a continuation of the concept of mediamorphosis based on the whole of cultural life see Alfred Smudits, *Mediamorphosen des Kulturschaffens: Kunst und Kommunikationstechnologien im Wandel* (Vienna: 2002).

70 Kurt Blaukopf, "Westernisation, Modernisation and the Mediamorphosis of Music", *International Review of the Aesthetics and Sociology of Music*, vol. 20, no. 2, 1989, 183–192; id., "Legal Policies for the Safeguarding of Traditional Music: Are they Utopian?" *The World of Music*, vol. 32, no. 1, 1990, 125–133.

71 cf. for example Kurt Blaukopf / Alfred Smudits, "Auswirkungen neuer Technologien auf das Kulturschaffen und den Status des Kulturschaffenden", *SWS-*

copyright law in the context of technological reproducibility,[72] with the influence of the TV screen on perception,[73] and with the secondary use of music in the media.[74] The starting point of the research is the observation of the divergence of the possibilities of artistic creation evoked by technological development on the one hand and the culture, media and educational policy conditions on the other. In this connection, William F. Ogburn's theory of cultural phase shift[75] finds an application in the cultural field. For Blaukopf, the term "cultural lag" describes the "process of delayed adaptation of elements of culture to rapidly changing circumstances, above all . . . of a technical nature".[76] The lagging of policy measures in the cultural sphere had to be made into an object of research. In this connection, the term "technology-consequences assessment" introduced a change of course in the Mediacult institute: in an article on the future tasks of Mediacult, Blaukopf advanced the thesis that under existing circumstances it was no longer sufficient to establish the potential consequences for culture of the changes in the media landscape, but that it had become necessary "to give clear signals that draw attention in good time to the bottlenecks or obstructions to cultural development".[77] The aim was to develop an early-warning system to be used by cultural policy, whose task was to identify the potential opportunities but also the dangers of the development of new communications technologies in good time.

Parallel to these considerations Blaukopf developed the concept of the "cultural market economy". In numerous texts[78] he called for a market

Rundschau, yr. 27, vol. 2, 1987, 243–247.

72 Kurt Blaukopf, *Strategies of music industries and radio organisations* (research report of the Council of Europe, 1985).

73 cf. for example Kurt Blaukopf, "Mensch und Bildschirm – Eine Lücke in der Wirkungsforschung", in Walter Nutz (ed.), *Kunst – Kultur – Kommunikation* (Frankfurt: 1989), 75–83.

74 Kurt Blaukopf, "Die sekundäre Nutzung von Musik in den Medien", *Orbis Musicae*, no. 9, 1986, 234–243.

75 William F. Ogburn, "Cultural Lag as Theory", *Sociology and Social Research*, 41/1957, 167–173.

76 Kurt Blaukopf, *Der Begriff des "cultural lag" in der "Mutationsforschung"*, (unpublished manuscript, s.a.), 1.

77 Kurt Blaukopf, "Ein Frühwarnsystem für die Kulturpolitik", *Unesco-Dienst*, yr. 33, no. 10, 1986, 13.

78 Kurt Blaukopf, "Musik in der Mediamorphose, Plädoyer für eine kulturelle Marktwirtschaft", *Media Perspektiven*, 9/1989, 552–558; Kurt Blaukopf / Her-

correction in the field of culture that would do justice to the tension between profit-oriented economics and the cultural requirements in the age of mediamorphosis. Following the terms "social market economy" and "ecological market economy", Blaukopf called for a "cultural market economy", which was indeed oriented on the principle of supply and demand, but at the same time countered tendencies that threatened the diversity of different musics. Blaukopf was here aware that these demands were based on specific value judgements. However, the disclosure of these specific values distinguishes him from numerous both technologically euphoric as well as culturally pessimistic cultural studies scholars and political decision-makers whose criteria for their societal diagnoses and prognoses seldom see the light of day.

Blaukopf gained a hearing in numerous journalistic contributions on culture and media policy also beyond academic periodicals and lists of cultural policy measures. In 1988 he was awarded the Austrian State Prize for Cultural Journalism.

Finally, mention should also be made of the book on the Vienna Philharmonic, published together with his wife Herta Blaukopf, in which the history of this orchestra is documented together with detailed image and text material.[79] The academic concern with the Vienna Philharmonic not only reflects Blaukopf's interest in concrete musical life, but is also considered to be a pioneering work in the field of Austrian orchestra research.

1990–1999: In Search of the Historical Development of Empirical Cultural Research in Austria

In the last years of his life, Kurt Blaukopf dedicated himself to an – ostensibly – completely new theme: as a member of the "Institute of the Vienna Circle" he concerned himself with the tradition of logical empiricism in Austria. On closer observation, however, it becomes evident that this subject is by no means foreign to Blaukopf. And there are two

---

mann Rauhe, "Kulturelle Marktwirtschaft als Antwort auf die Mediamorphose", in Hermann Rauhe et al. (eds.), *Kulturmanagement: Theorie und Praxis einer professionellen Kunst* (Berlin: 1994), 91–100.

79 Herta Blaukopf / Kurt Blaukopf, *Die Wiener Philharmoniker: Wesen, Werden, Wirken eines großen Orchesters* (Vienna: 1986).

reasons for this: On the one hand, as head of the project on "The Scientific World Conception and Art", Kurt Blaukopf was researching the historical line of development of empirical cultural research in Austria – and in the process was tracing the development of music sociology. On the other hand the concern with this variant of Austrian philosophy represented a continuation of an interest that he had already cherished in his student years and that had been a constantly recurring interest in the course of his activity as a music sociologist.[80]

The "Vienna Circle" is the name of the academic group of the 1920s and 1930s whose principal aim was a fundamental reshaping of philosophy against the background of a positivist approach: members included a range of Austrian physicians, mathematicians and philosophers who, following Ernst Mach's empirio-criticism concerned themselves with the role of empiricism in the process of perception – and ultimately coined the term "logical empiricism".[81] In the programme of the Vienna Circle *Wissenschaftliche Weltauffassung – der Wiener Kreis* in 1929, Otto Neurath, Rudolf Carnap and Hans Hahn[82] formulated the basic positions of logical empiricism. The starting point of this "scientific world conception" is the radical rejection of any metaphysics: this approach is based the assumption of experience as the only source of knowledge: "there is no way to genuine knowledge other than the way of experience; there is no realm of ideas that stands over or beyond experience."[83] Criticism is above all directed at the speculative aspect of philosophy: only empirical observation alone could form the basis of any scientific knowledge. Alongside the anti-metaphysical approach, the orientation on the natural sciences was the second pillar of the Vienna Circle: Neurath and Carnap called for the "search for a

---

80 On Blaukopf's relationship to the Vienna Circle in the first half of the century see Friedrich Stadler: "'Wissenschaftliche Weltauffassung und Kunst': Kurt Blaukopf und die österreichische Philosophie", in Martin Seiler / Friedrich Stadler (eds.), *Kunst, Kunsttheorie und Kunstforschung im wissenschaftlichen Diskurs* (Vienna: 2000), 20–34.

81 Other terms are "logical positivism", "neo-positivism" and "analytical philosophy".

82 Otto Neurath / Rudolf Carnap, "The Scientific Conception of the World: The Vienna Circle", in Sahotra Sarkar (ed.), *Science and Philosophy in the Twentieth Century: Basic Works of Logical Empiricism, Vol. 1. The Emergence of Logical Empiricism: From 1900 to the Vienna Circle* (New York/ London: 1996), 321–340.

83 ibid. 338.

neutral system of formulae, for a symbolism freed from the slag of historical languages; and also the search for a total system of concepts".[84] This formal logical system might correspond to the instrument that is above all already present in physics and mathematics, since it a question of striving for "accuracy and clarity" and above all freedom from contradiction. The demand to present complex circumstances in the framework of a mathematical concept apparatus that was as simple and transparent as possible has to be seen in the context of a further epistemological aim of the Vienna Circle. It was Otto Neurath above all who endeavoured to establish a kind of universal language of science: "The endeavour is to link and harmonise the achievements of individual investigators in their various fields of science."[85] This programme of an integrated science by no means – as is often assumed – pursued the aim of tracing the laws of all sciences back to the laws of one science (e.g. physics), but to express scientific knowledge within a shared unifying epistemology.

During his period in exile Blaukopf had concerned himself intensively with the uniqueness of Austrian intellectual life – which also includes art and the traditions of philosophy. An article published in *Zeitspiegel* in 1945 mentions the "specific Austrian tradition in the way of approaching philosophical problems".[86] It outlines the precursors of the tradition of thought that was later under the name of the "Vienna Circle" to play a central role in Blaukopf's understanding of music sociology. At the end of this article Blaukopf called for attention to "the unique development of philosophical thought in Austria. A thorough investigation of these questions would represent an important contribution to the study of Austrian history and cultural history".[87]

Fifty years later, Kurt Blaukopf took up this project, which he had already been planning in the 1940s: in the framework of the project on "The Scientific World Conception and Art", Blaukopf concerned himself with the empiricist tradition of Austrian music and art research, which can be traced back to the era of late Josephinism. His book

84 ibid., 328.
85 ibid., 328.
86 Kurt Blaukopf, "Zur Geschichte der Philosophie in Österreich I", *Zeitspiegel*, 16.6.1945.
87 Kurt Blaukopf, "Zur Geschichte der Philosophie in Österreich II", *Zeitspiegel*, 25.8.1945.

Pioniere empiristischer Musikforschung [Pioneers of Empiricist Music Research] presents the diverse approaches of Johann Friedrich Herbart, Bernard Bolzano, Eduard Hanslick, Ernst Mach, Alois Riegl, Richard Wallaschek, Guido Adler and many more who had made an important contribution to the development of a specifically Austrian school of the sociology of the arts.[88] The starting point for this research is the empiricist tradition of the Vienna Circle, in which Blaukopf sees a crystallising point of these important methodological approaches.

In numerous other writings Blaukopf dealt with the individual representatives of empiricist arts research – here Bernard Bolzano, Leo Wilzin, Otto Neurath, Robert Zimmermann and Karl Popper should be mentioned. From 1992 to 1994 he engaged in correspondence with Popper[89] that provides information on Blaukopf's basic positivist approach. Thus Blaukopf writes to Popper about his concern with the empiricist tradition in music research: "It was (and is) my concern to apply the importance of the discoveries of Karl Popper also to my research area in order to dispel the shadows cast by speculative sociologism. . . . It is my concern to reveal the historical roots of a 'situation-analytical' sociology that is oriented on the methods of the natural sciences."[90]

The awarding of an honorary doctorate in 1994 "filled me with gratitude", wrote Blaukopf, "because I see in it, for me at least, an important step to the meaningful incorporation of my discipline in the encyclopaedia of the sciences".[91] This sentence comes from his autobiography and collected texts *Unterwegs zur Musiksoziologie* [On the Way to Music Sociology], published in 1998, in which Blaukopf outlines the rocky path from his first music-sociological thoughts in the 1930s to the establishment of this subject as an independent discipline.

Kurt Blaukopf died on 14 June 1999. The last of his articles prepared for publication (which only appeared posthumously) is entitled "Musik-

---

88 Kurt Blaukopf, *Pioniere empiristischer Musikforschung: Österreich und Böhmen als Wiege der modernen Kunstsoziologie*, series "Wissenschaftliche Weltauffassung und Kunst" vol. 1 (Vienna: 1995).
89 Published in Martin Seiler / Friedrich Stadler (eds.), *Kunst, Kunsttheorie und Kunstforschung im wissenschaftlichen Diskurs: In memoriam Kurt Blaukopf (1914-1999)* (Vienna: 2000), 251–274.
90 ibid., 254.
91 Kurt Blaukopf, *Unterwegs zur Musiksoziologie*, op.cit., 85.

praxis als Gegenstand der Soziologie" [Music Praxis as a Subject of Sociology].[92] It concerns a text that was written 30 years previously and exists in a handwritten version.[93] This text contains a precise exposition of Blaukopf's music sociology summarised in ca. 100 paragraphs. It reflects Blaukopf's close relationship to the philosophy of science of the Vienna Circle: at the same time, these notes clarify Blaukopf's early abilities as an impartial observer, an assiduous thinker and a far-sighted scientist. His approach to a range of questions that decisively shaped the 20th century suggests retrospectively awarding him the label that was originally applied to Gustav Mahler: a "contemporary of the future".[94]

92 Kurt Blaukopf, "Musikpraxis als Gegenstand der Soziologie", in Michael Benedikt / Reinhold Knoll / Kurt Lüthi (eds), *Über Gesellschaft hinaus: Kultursoziologische Beiträge im Gedenken an Robert Heinrich Reichardt* (Klausen-Leopoldsdorf: 2000), 145–161. Published also in this anthology, see page 21–35.
93 Kurt Blaukopf, *Ruskamen 1969* (unpublished manuscript, 1969).
94 Kurt Blaukopf, *Gustav Mahler oder Der Zeitgenosse der Zukunft* (Vienna et al.: 1969).

Appendix

Selected list of publications of Kurt Blaukopf

A complete documentation of Blaukopf's ouevre is published in: Institut für Musiksoziologie (ed.), *Fast eine Biografie: Kurt Blaukopf in seinen Schriften* (Strasshof: 1999).

Monographies

Musiksoziologie: Eine Einführung in die Grundbegriffe mit besonderer Berücksichtigung der Soziologie der Tonsysteme (Vienna: 1950).

Musik der "einsamen Masse": Ein Beitrag zur Analyse von Schlagerschallplatten, series "Musik und Gesellschaft" vol. 4 (Karlsruhe: 1968), (together with Gunnar Sonstevold).

Gustav Mahler oder Der Zeitgenosse der Zukunft (Vienna et al.: 1969), published in English: *Gustav Mahler* (London: 1973).

Neue musikalische Verhaltensweisen der Jugend, series "Musikpädagogik Forschung und Lehre" vol. 5 (Mainz: 1974).

Beethovens Erben in der Mediamorphose: Kultur-und Medienpolitik für die elektronische Ära (Heiden: 1989).

Musik im Wandel der Gesellschaft: Grundzüge der Musiksoziologie (Munich: 1982, second extended edition Darmstadt: 1996); published in English: *Musical Life in a Changing Society: Aspects of Music Sociology* (Portland: 1992).

Pioniere empiristischer Musikforschung: Österreich und Böhmen als Wiege der modernen Kunstsoziologie, series "Wissenschaftliche Weltauffassung und Kunst" vol. 1 (Vienna: 1995).

Editor

Philosophie, Literatur und Musik im Orchester der Wissenschaften (Vienna: 1996).

Articles in books and academic journals

"Raumakustische Probleme der Musiksoziologie", *Gravesaner Blätter*, 5/1960, 163–173.

"Westernisation, Modernisation and the Mediamorphosis of Music", *International Review of the Aesthetics and Sociology of Music*, vol. 20, no. 2, 1989, 183–192.

"Kunstsoziologie im Orchester der Wissenschaften", in Alfred Smudits / Helmut Staubmann (eds.), *Kunst Geschichte Soziologie: Beiträge zur soziologischen Kunstbetrachtung aus Österreich, Festschrift für Gerhard Kapner* (Frankfurt am Main: 1997), 21–32.

"Kunstforschung als exakte Wissenschaft: Von Diderot zur Enzyklopädie des Wiener Kreises", in Friedrich Stadler (ed.), *Elemente moderner Wissenschaftstheorie* (Vienna/New York: 1999), 177–210.

"Musik und Musiksoziologie im Werk Karl Poppers", in Wolfgang Lipp (ed.), *Gesellschaft und Musik: Wege zur Musiksoziologie*, Sociologia Internationalis, supplement 1 (Berlin: 1992), 161–183.

"Musikpraxis als Gegenstand der Soziologie", in Michael Benedikt / Reinhold Knoll / Kurt Lüthi (eds.), *Über Gesellschaft hinaus: Kultursoziologische Beiträge im Gedenken an Robert Heinrich Reichardt* (Klausen-Leoplodsdorf: 2000), 145–161.

Anthologies of texts by Kurt Blaukopf

Kurt Blaukopf, *Unterwegs zur Musiksoziologie. Auf der Suche nach Heimat und Standort*, kommentiert von Reinhard Müller, series "Bibliothek sozialwissenschaftlicher Emigranten" vol. 4 (Graz/Vienna: 1998).

Kurt Blaukopf, *Was ist Musiksoziologie? Ausgewählte Texte*, Michael Parzer (ed.), series "Musik und Gesellschaft" vol. 28 (Frankfurt am Main: 2010).

Publications on the oeuvre of Kurt Blaukopf

Irmgard Bontinck (ed.), *Wege zu einer Wiener Schule der Musiksoziologie: Konvergenz der Disziplinen und empiristische Tradition* (Vienna/Mühlheim a. d. Ruhr: 1996).

Peter K. Etzkorn, "Music and its Audience: Reflections on Blaukopf's Sociology and Implications for Music Education in the United States", *Musikerziehung*, 53, yr. 2000, 137–147.

Michael Parzer, "Soziologie, Kulturwissenschaft und die Wiener Schule der Musiksoziologie: Ein Plädoyer für die Interdisziplinarität musiksoziologischer Forschung", in Michael Parzer (ed.), *Musiksoziologie remixed: Impulse aus dem aktuellen kulturwissenschaftlichen Diskurs* (Vienna: 2004), 9–15.

Alfred Smudits, "Zur Produktion von Kultur – österreichische und US-amerikanische Ansätze", in Tasos Zembylas / Peter Tschmuck (eds.), *Kulturbetriebsforschung: Ansätze und Perspektiven der Kulturbetriebslehre* (Wiesbaden: 2006), 63–76.

Friedrich Stadler, "'Wissenschaftliche Weltauffassung und Kunst': Kurt Blaukopf und die österreichische Philosophie", in Martin Seiler/Friedrich Stadler (eds.): *Kunst, Kunsttheorie und Kunstforschung im wissenschaftlichen Diskurs* (Vienna: 2000), 20–34.

The Kurt Blaukopf Archive in Vienna

The Kurt Blaukopf Archive was opened in 2007 and is administered by the Institute for Music Sociology at the University of Music and Performing Arts Vienna. The aim of the archive is the systematic collecting and classification of the writings of Kurt Blaukopf. The archive is open to the public and has an online database – see http://www.mdw.ac.at/ims/?PageId=2081.

It includes approximately 1,600 texts (thereof 150 scientific articles, 850 contributions to newspapers and magazines), 300 record reviews and 300 unpublished manuscripts. Above and beyond this there is a bundle of correspondence, recordings and audiovisual material.

Copyright permissions

Musik und Gesellschaft

„Musik und Gesellschaft" begründet 1967 von Kurt Blaukopf.

Heft 1-21 herausgegeben von Kurt Blaukopf

Heft 1 Gottfried von Einem: Komponist und Gesellschaft. Verlag G. Braun. Karlsruhe 1967.

Heft 2 Zur Bestimmung der klanglichen Erfahrung der Musikstudierenden. Ein Forschungsbericht. Verlag G. Braun. Karlsruhe 1968.

Heft 3 Kurt Blaukopf: Werktreue und Bearbeitung. Zur Soziologie der Integrität des musikalischen Kunstwerks. Verlag G. Braun. Karlsruhe 1968.

Heft 4 Gunnar Sønstevold / Kurt Blaukopf: Musik der „einsamen Masse". Ein Beitrag zur Analyse von Schlagerschallplatten. Verlag G. Braun. Karlsruhe 1968.

Heft 5 Karel Pech: Hören im „optischen Zeitalter". Verlag G. Braun. Karlsruhe 1969.

Heft 6 Walter Graf: Die musikalische Klangforschung. Wege zur Erfassung der musikalischen Bedeutung der Klangfarbe. Verlag G. Braun. Karlsruhe 1969.

Heft 7/8 Technik, Wirtschaft und Ästhetik der Schallplatte. Symposion auf der hifi '68 Düsseldorf". Verlag G. Braun. Karlsruhe 1970.

Heft 9 Dieter Zimmerschied: Gesucht: Das Volkslied. Schüleruntersuchungen über die Stellung des Volksliedes im Bewußtsein verschiedener Bevölkerungsgruppen in Mainz und Umgebung. Verlag G. Braun. Karlsruhe 1971.

Heft 10/11 Hans-Peter Reinecke et al.: High Fidelity und Stereophonie – ihr Platz und Rang im Musikleben. Symposion auf der „hifi ‚70 Düsseldorf'. Verlag G. Braun. Karlsruhe 1971.

Heft 12 Luigi del Grosso Destreri: Europäisches Hit-Panorama. Erfolgsschlager in vier europäischen Ländern 1964 und 1967. Aussagen, Inhalte, Analysen. Verlag G. Braun. Karlsruhe 1972.

Heft 13/14 Hermann Rauhe: Popularität in der Musik. Interdisziplinäre Aspekte musikalischer Kommunikation. Verlag G. Braun. Karlsruhe 1974.

Heft 15 Wilrich Hoffmann: Komponist und Technik. Die Bedeutung naturwissenschaftlicher Forschung für die Musik. Verlag G. Braun. Karlsruhe 1975.

Heft 16 Robert Wangermée: Rundfunkmusik gegen die Kulturmoralisten verteidigt. Versuch zur künstlerischen Kommunikation. Verlag G. Braun. Karlsruhe 1975.

Heft 17 Kurt Blaukopf et al.: Soziographie des Musiklebens. Beiträge zur Datensammlung und Methodik. Verlag G. Braun. Karlsruhe 1979.

Heft 18 Karl Breh: Die Mutation musikalischer Kommunikation durch High Fidelity und Stereophonie. Verlag G. Braun. Karlsruhe 1980.

Heft 19 Desmond Mark: John H. Mueller – Ein Pionier der Musiksoziologie. Verlag des Verbandes der wissenschaftlichen Gesellschaften Österreichs. Wien 1985.

Heft 20 Massenmedien, Musikpolitik und Musikerziehung. Herausgegeben von Elena Ostleitner. Verlag des Verbandes der wissenschaftlichen Gesellschaften Österreichs. Wien 1987.

Heft 21 Desmond Mark: Musikschule 2000. Der Bedarf an Musikschullehrern. Bestandsaufnahme, Berufsbild, Prognose. Verlag des Verbandes der wissenschaftlichen Gesellschaften Österreichs. Wien 1990.

Heft 22, Band 23-27 herausgegeben von Irmgard Bontinck

Heft   22   Kulturpolitik, Kunst, Musik. Fragen an die Soziologie. Herausgegeben von Irmgard Bontinck. Verlag des Verbandes der wissenschaftlichen Gesellschaften Österreichs. Wien 1992.

Band   23   Wege zu einer Wiener Schule der Musiksoziologie. Konvergenz der Disziplinen und empiristische Tradition. Herausgegeben von Irmgard Bontinck. Verlag Guthmann-Peterson. Wien-Mühlheim a. d. Ruhr 1996.

Band   24   Paul Lazarsfelds Wiener RAVAG-Studie 1932. Der Beginn der modernen Rundfunkforschung. Herausgegeben von Desmond Mark. Verlag Guthmann-Peterson. Wien-Mühlheim a. d. Ruhr 1996.

Band   25   Jazz als Ereignis und Konserve. Herausgegeben von Alfred Smudits und Heinz Steinert. Verlag Guthmann-Peterson. Wien-Mühlheim a. d. Ruhr 1997.

Band   26   Desmond Mark: Wem gehört der Konzertsaal? Das Wiener Orchesterrepertoire im internationalen Vergleich. Zur Frage des musikalischen Geschmacks bei John H. Mueller. Verlag Guthmann-Peterson. Wien-Mühlheim a. d. Ruhr 1998.

Band   27   Alfred Smudits: Mediamorphosen des Kulturschaffens. Kunst und Kommunikationstechnologien im Wandel. Verlag Braumüller. Wien 2002.

ab Band 28 herausgegeben von Alfred Smudits im Verlag Peter Lang

Band   28   Kurt Blaukopf: Was ist Musiksoziologie? Ausgewählte Texte. Herausgegeben von Michael Parzer. 2010.

Band   29   Alenka Barber-Kersovan / Harald Huber / Alfred Smudits (Hrsg.): West Meets East. Musik im interkulturellen Dialog. 2011.

Band   30   Michael Parzer: Der gute Musikgeschmack. Zur sozialen Praxis ästhetischer Bewertung in der Popularkultur. 2011.

Band   31   Tasos Zembylas (ed.): Kurt Blaukopf on Music Sociology – an Anthology. Edited by Tasos Zembylas. 2012. 2. Auflage 2016.

Band   32   Noraldine Bailer / Christian Glanz (Hrsg.): Musikbildung – Allgemeinbildung. Gewidmet Alfred Litschauer. 2012.

Band   33   Susanne Binas-Preisendörfer / Melanie Unseld (Hrsg.): Transkulturalität und Musikvermittlung. Möglichkeiten und Herausforderungen in Forschung, Kulturpolitik und musikpädagogischer Praxis. Unter Mitarbeit von Sophie Arenhövel. 2012.

Band   34   Andreas Gebesmair / Anja Brunner / Regina Sperlich: Balkanboom! Eine Geschichte der Balkanmusik in Österreich. 2014.

Band   35   Martin Niederauer: Die Widerständigkeiten des Jazz. Sozialgeschichte und Improvisation unter den Imperativen der Kulturindustrie. 2014.

www.peterlang.com

www.ingramcontent.com/pod-product-compliance
Lightning Source LLC
Chambersburg PA
CBHW070812300326
41914CB00054B/778